EXPERIENCE INTO WORDS

EXPERIENCE INTO WORDS

D. W. Harding

EMERITUS PROFESSOR OF PSYCHOLOGY IN
THE UNIVERSITY OF LONDON

CAMBRIDGE UNIVERSITY PRESS

CAMBRIDGE

LONDON   NEW YORK   NEW ROCHELLE

MELBOURNE   SYDNEY

Published by the Press Syndicate of the University of Cambridge
The Pitt Building, Trumpington Street, Cambridge CB2 1RP
32 East 57th Street, New York, NY 10022, USA
296 Beaconsfield Parade, Middle Park, Melbourne 3206, Australia

First published by Chatto and Windus 1963
First paperback edition published by Cambridge University Press 1982

Printed in Great Britain at the
University Press, Cambridge

Library of Congress catalogue card number: 81–10056

British Library cataloguing in publication data

Harding, D. W.
Experience into words.
1. English poetry – Addresses, essays, lectures.
I. Title
821′.009   PR504
ISBN 0 521 28543 7

Contents

To
R. McArthur

Foreword

THE essays brought together here deal with the relation between the writer's words and some other, non-literary experience, whether his or his readers'. It is a dangerous area of interest, which comes and goes in fashion according as one of two errors becomes more evident: the first, forgetting that the understanding of a poem (by the author or his readers) is an experience quite distinct from any other experiences on which its creation and understanding may depend; the second, neglecting the requirement that the poem should be anchored closely enough in comprehended sense for the writer and the reader to be relating it to the same kind of other experiences. The first error leads to an undue preoccupation with the poem's paraphrasable meaning (with a grossly oversimplified view of the way poems work), and perhaps to irrelevant biographical assumptions about the author's experience. The opposite error tempts poets to trade in sham incantation and gestures of profundity and encourages their readers to rest content with idiosyncratic interpretation or the elementary pleasures of the higher babble.

Between these two errors we all want, naturally, to keep a perfect balance—but who can? I lean towards the first, without, I hope, falling. To me it seems that criticism has still not benefited enough from I. A. Richards' striking demonstration, years ago, of the ease with which intelligent people misconstrue or fail to grasp the 'sense' of poems. Several of these essays, therefore, are attempts to understand what the poet is talking about. That sometimes means examining themes that can be seen only in a broad survey (as in the discussion of Donne's poems and Eliot's plays), and it sometimes calls for a closer study of the way the poet is using his words and statements. The task presents special difficulty and interest if the poetry is the kind that gains much of its effect from overtones of meaning and hinted symbolism without explicit allegory. It is when poets are working in this way that we can see most clearly the influence on their thought of the language and imagery in which it takes form. This is the theme of the last essay, 'The Hinterland of Thought'; it sets in a more general context the broad problem of which various aspects have appeared in the studies of particular writers.

Most of these essays have appeared before and I am grateful to publishers and editors for permission to reprint them: to Kenyon College and the Editors of *The Kenyon Review* for 'Donne's Anticipation of Experience' and 'Progression of Theme in Eliot's Modern Plays'; to Penguin Books and Professor Boris Ford, General Editor of *The Pelican Guide to English Literature*, for 'Experience and Symbol in Blake'; to the Editors of *Scrutiny* for 'The Theme of The Ancient Mariner', 'Aspects of the Poetry of Isaac Rosenberg', 'Words and Meanings: A Note on Eliot's Poetry', and 'The Changed Outlook in Eliot's Later Poems'; to the Colston Research Society, Butterworths, and Professor L. C. Knights and Dr Basil Cottle, Editors of *Metaphor and Symbol* (Vol. XII of the Colston Papers) for 'The Hinterland of Thought'. The passage from Salvador de Madariaga, *Don Quixote*, in 'Reader and Author' is quoted by kind permission of The Clarendon Press, Oxford.

My greatest debt is to Dr F. R. Leavis, who encouraged my early work; *Scrutiny*, which he kept going in face of great difficulties and intense hostility, gave me for many years the only opportunity I had of publishing what I wrote.

1

Donne's Anticipation of Experience

HARDY has a poem, 'The Self-Unseeing', in which he records a scene that appears in retrospect as one of the moments of value in life but was not at the time experienced vividly at its worth—'Yet we were looking away!' In Donne's work there occurs curiously often, in several different forms, an attempted insurance against some such failure of experience. In one of its forms it shows as a prolonged effort of anticipation, as though to ensure full responsiveness to the event when it did come. In the early work, of course, the long-drawn-out anticipation is of sexual experience; and this gives the broad pattern of the zestfully sensual poems, 'To his Mistris going to bed' and 'Whoever loves, if he do not propose The right true end of love'. The Epithalamions also served him well (apart from their social and pecuniary value) because they invited this process of leading up to the experience with an 'impatient' anticipation that allows him to dwell longer and more vividly on the idea of sexual union, and because they justified by the conventions of the occasion the onlooker's rather mental preoccupation with sexuality that goes with such anticipation. But in later poems, as I must come to consider, the same anticipation is applied to the act of dying.

Another form of insurance against failing of full response to the significant event is seen in Donne's fantasy that the moment of experience can be immensely protracted:

> All day, the same our postures were,
> And wee said nothing, all the day.

'The Computation' uses a similar exaggeration more light-heartedly:

> For the first twenty yeares, since yesterday,
>   I scarce beleev'd, thou could'st be gone away,
> For forty more, I fed on favours past,
>   And forty'on hopes, that thou would'st, they might last.
> Teares drown'd one hundred, and sighes blew out two . . .

and so on through several thousand years.

Donne's affirmation in 'The Extasie' that 'no change can invade' the materials of the lovers' united soul illustrates his turning to love as a further means of counteracting his sense of the transience of satisfying experience. The long build-up to an awaited event was one means; the notion of an immensely protracted moment of time was another. And now a third, more directly aimed at a denial of the fact, was this fantasy of time arrested through love and the process of decay interdicted. 'The Anniversarie' states it:

> Only our love hath no decay;
> This, no to morrow hath, nor yesterday,
> Running it never runs from us away,
> But truly keeps his first, last, everlasting day.

In 'Loves Growth', again, although the ordinary process of growth in nature is used at first as an analogy with the increase of his love in spring, the equally inevitable decay is denied:

> And though each spring doe adde to love new heate,
>
> .   .   .   .   .
>
> No winter shall abate the springs encrease.

This fantasy brings him nearest to convinced comfort and is associated with his rare spells of belief in complete security of affection, as in 'The Anniversarie':

> Who is so safe as wee? where none can doe
> Treason to us, except one of us two.

12

Yet the quick glance even here at the possibility that treason *might* come, from 'one of us two', is characteristic. So too, in 'A Lecture upon the Shadow', Donne gives a warning even while he tries to convey his conviction of their security in love:

> Except our loves at this noone stay,
> We shall new shadowes make the other way.
> > As the first were made to blinde
> > Others; these which come behinde
> Will worke upon our selves, and blind our eyes.
> If our loves faint, and westwardly decline;
> > To me thou, falsly, thine,
> > And I to thee mine actions shall disguise.

The fear of betrayal, and possibly mutual betrayal, creeps in, and instead of affirming the permanence of love he can only demand it:

> The morning shadowes weare away,
> But these grow longer all the day,
> But oh, loves day is short, if love decay.
>
> Love is a growing, or full constant light;
> And his first minute, after noone, is night.

Fantasies of permanence and demands for it are alike the occasional denials of what he was chiefly aware of, the impossibility of seizing the satisfying state of experience and keeping it. He develops the theme in 'The Second Anniversary':

> And what essentiall joy can'st thou expect
> Here upon earth? what permanent effect
> Of transitory causes? Doest thou love
> Beauty? (And beauty worthy'st is to move)
> Poore cousened cousenor, *that* she, and *that* thou,
> Which did begin to love, are neither now;
> You are both fluid, chang'd since yesterday;

Next day repaires, (but ill) last dayes decay.
Nor are, (although the river keepe the name)
Yesterdaies waters, and to daies the same.
So flowes her face, and thine eyes . . .

The poems of permanence in love provide a brief contrast with both earlier and later expressions of protest at the transience of what he values. Elegy X, 'The Dreame', gives an early statement of the theme:

But dearest heart, and dearer image stay;
Alas, true joyes at best are *dreame* enough;
Though you stay here you passe too fast away:
For even at first lifes *Taper* is a snuffe.

And much later in life, in Holy Sonnet VI, contemplating the short time still before him—'this last pace'—he brings together both the brevity of life and his conviction of having failed to use it worthily in the concise words

. . . my race
Idly, yet quickly runne, hath this last pace.

Not only is the longed for experience transient, it is disappointing too. Elegy XV, 'The Expostulation', states explicitly the use to which he puts postponement:

Now have I curst, let us our love revive;
In mee the flame was never more alive;
I could beginne againe to court and praise,
And in that pleasure lengthen the short dayes
Of my lifes lease; like Painters that do take
Delight, not in made worke, but whiles they make.

The idea of lengthening life by the delays and anticipations of courtship provides a complete contrast with Marvell's attitude in the poem 'To His Coy Mistress'. There, the brevity of life is a reason for contracting the courtship and pressing on to the final experience; here, with Donne, the brevity of life is felt most in the transience of the moment of experience, and life is therefore lengthened by delay and anticipation. But Donne goes even further by suggesting that the anticipation is more rewarding than the event:

> . . . like Painters that do take
> Delight, not in made worke, but whiles they make.

It comes then as no surprise to meet such poems as 'Farewell to Love', with its theme of disappointment in sexual experience, or 'Loves Alchymie', in which the disillusionment seems to be still more strongly felt:

> Some that have deeper digg'd loves Myne than I,
> Say, where his centrique happinesse doth lie:
>   I have lov'd, and got, and told,
> But should I love, get, tell, till I were old,
> I should not finde that hidden mysterie;
>   Oh, 'tis imposture all:
> And as no chymique yet th'Elixar got,
>   But glorifies his pregnant pot,
>   If by the way to him befall
> Some odoriferous thing, or medicinall,
>   So, lovers dreame a rich and long delight,
>   But get a winter-seeming summers night.

*   *   *   *   *

It seems reasonable to think that Donne's elaborate building up towards an experience was associated with some anxiety about the worth of the event when it actually came or about the adequacy of his own response to it. This may seem an odd suspicion to harbour of Donne, if we accept too simple an idea of the early poems as expressing an immense zest and gusto in sexual enjoyment. In fact the gusto turns out to be mainly in the anticipation. And there is not so complete a contrast of mood as a first glance might suggest between the early writing and the later religious poems. It is true that in 'The Litanie' (III) he speaks of himself, on rather conventional lines, as being

> Halfe wasted with youths fires, of pride and lust,

and says in Holy Sonnet V of the 'little world' which is himself that

> . . . the fire
> Of lust and envie have burnt it heretofore.

This confirms the simplest impression of the early poems. But a far fuller and carefully introspective account of his early troubles is given in Holy Sonnet III; and here, perhaps to our surprise, we find that the early sins he accuses himself of are grief and despair:

> In mine Idolatry what showres of raine
> Mine eyes did waste? what griefs my heart did rent?
> That sufferance was my sinne; now I repent;
> 'Cause I did suffer I must suffer paine.
> Th'hydroptique drunkard, and night-scouting thiefe,
> The itchy Lecher, and selfe tickling proud
> Have the remembrance of past joyes, for reliefe
> Of comming ills. To (poore) me is allow'd
> No ease; for, long, yet vehement griefe hath beene
> Th'effect and cause, the punishment and sinne.

This is a clear and considered statement that the pride and lust, of which he accuses himself in other poems, gave him none of the expected gratifications even at the time, and that he now blames himself for the protests and grief of his early life. There can be no reason for ignoring this reflective and explicit account. Taken seriously, it heightens the significance of the early poems of disillusionment.

I want to ask why the experiences of living failed to give Donne what they had seemed to promise and why he felt that the satisfying states of experience slipped away before he was ready to let them go. He himself gives the answer quite clearly, if we are willing to accept it, in 'An Anatomie of the World', a poem that treats directly of the defects and disillusionments of human life. 'The First Anniversary' gives an extraordinarily thorough catalogue of the unworthiness of men as they are, a catalogue of self-contempt, contrasting the puny, mentally shrunken and short-lived creatures that we are with the promise held out by the primitive world in the days of Methuselah and our gigantic forbears. That catalogue completed, Donne restates his opening theme of supreme loss through the death of the idealized woman whom he chose to represent by Elizabeth Drury. To his contemporaries' protest (echoed by some modern critics) at the grotesque over-idealization of this young girl whom he had never met, Donne replied quite plainly that his purpose was 'to say, not what I was sure was just truth, but the best that I could conceive', and (according to Jonson) 'that he described the Idea of a Woman, and not as she was'. As Jonson pointed out, he comes very near ascribing the merits of the Virgin Mary to the unfortunate girl:

> Shee in whom vertue was so much refin'd,
> That for Allay unto so pure a minde
> Shee tooke the weaker Sex; shee that could drive
> The poysonous tincture, and the staine of *Eve*,
> Out of her thoughts, and deeds; and purifie
> All, by a true religious Alchymie.

Significantly, he attributes to her not merely freedom from sexual interest but also intuitive omniscience—

> Shee who all libraries had throughly read
> At home in her owne thoughts.

and a limitless power for good:

> This is the worlds condition now, and now
> Shee that should all parts to reunion bow,
> Shee that had all Magnetique force alone,

17

> To draw, and fasten sundred parts in one; . . .
> Shee that was best, and first originall
> Of all faire copies, and the generall
> Steward to Fate; shee whose rich eyes, and breast
> Guilt the West Indies, and perfum'd the East . . .

Jonson seems amply justified in feeling that this was not merely a virgin but a virgin mother.

Given our own unworthiness as men, compared to our forbears, Donne sees our separation from this fantasied perfection of woman as the final reason for despair at the world's imperfections. While she was with us there was hope:

> . . . in all shee did,
> Some Figure of the Golden times was hid.

But now:

> Shee, shee is gone; shee is gone; when thou knowest this,
> What fragmentary rubbidge this world is
> Thou knowest.

Donne himself, therefore, accounts for the disappointing quality of human existence as he saw it by the loss of the perfectly satisfactory woman who has the attributes of divine motherhood. Such good as there is in the world derives solely from her:

> Though shee which did inanimate and fill
> The world, be gone, yet in this last long night,
> Her Ghost doth walke; that is, a glimmering light,
> A faint weake love of vertue, and of good,
> Reflects from her, on them which understood
> Her worth.

It seems to me that in the fantasy he created around Elizabeth Drury Donne expressed unwittingly the familiar psychological theme that for many people, of whom he was one, an unwilling and protesting separation from the fantasy-perfect mother of infancy leaves the world a permanently disappointing place. One may perhaps think that so much emphasis on the importance of the early mother-image and the loss of union with such a figure is a suspiciously unheralded importation into modern thought. But in fact even the conscious formulation of the idea occurs long before the introduction of psychoanalysis, as one sees in the following effusive passage from De Quincey:

> The bewildering romance, light tarnished with darkness, the semi-fabulous legend, truth celestial mixed with human falsehoods, these fade even of themselves as life advances. The romance has perished that the young man adored; the legend has gone that deluded the boy; but the deep, deep tragedies of infancy, as when the child's hands were unlinked for ever from his mother's neck, or his lips for ever from his mother's kisses, these remain lurking below all, and these lurk to the last.

Given abstract statement in an adult setting, the tragedies of infancy seem too slight and distant for the upsurge of emotion that De Quincey tries to release. The intense importance of infantile experience can rarely be felt with conviction in so direct a way (outside the psychoanalytic situation). It generally finds expression obliquely through an intellectually more mature idea. Thus the adoration of the Virgin Mary or of Kuan Yin allows the worshipper to feel something of the intensity of the infant's devotion to the mother—and to feel it reasonably, given faith in the religious system that establishes a child-mother ratio between devotee and cult figure. Donne's theme was ostensibly different; but the seemingly exaggerated emotion and boundless enlargement of the sense of loss occasioned by Elizabeth Drury's death can be understood if we take them as belonging to the hidden theme. We might try to discount the significance of 'An Anatomie of the World' by simply saying that Donne worked in a convention of eulogy that permitted exaggeration; but the crucial fact is that he broke the conventions of such an occasion and incurred complaints in his own time and ever since of having gone far beyond the limits of allowable eulogy. At all events, if we accept what he plainly states, he had the impulse at the age of thirty-nine to attribute the defects of the world and his disillusionment with human existence to the loss of the greatest perfection of womanhood of which he could conceive.

* * * * *

It then comes as no surprise to see what divided feelings his poems express towards the women around him. There is first the sharp contrast between women in their sexual and in their idealized maternal aspects; on the one hand, the women of some of the satires and simple sexual poems, and on the other the high-minded patronesses to whom he offers his cultured respect, such as Mrs Herbert:

> Here, where still *Evening* is; not *noone*, nor *night*;
> Where no *voluptuousnesse*, yet all *delight*.

In the latter category come the women whom he loves or pretends to love but whose faithfulness to other men wins his rueful respect. Thus in 'Twicknam Garden':

> O perverse sexe, where none is true but shee,
> Who's therefore true, because her truth kills mee.

and in 'Loves Deitie':

> Rebell and Atheist too, why murmure I,
> As though I felt the worst that love could doe?
> Love might make me leave loving, or might trie
> A deeper plague, to make her love mee too,
> Which, since she loves before, I'am loth to see;
> Falshood is worse than hate; and that must bee,
> If shee whom I love, should love mee.

But the possibility at least occurs to him that even the chaste and untouchable figure might have been accessible, as a variant stanza (in the 1635 edition) of 'The Curse' shows:

> Or may he for her vertue reverence
> One that hates him onely for impotence,
> And equall Traitors be she and his sense.

(Those who like psychoanalytic speculation will notice that this stanza was alternative to one that refers directly to incest.)

More frequently, the early poems deal with his sense of rejection and betrayal by the ordinary women with admitted sexual appetite. 'Loves Diet' presents the familiar sour-grapes device, an unconvincing defiance and a claim to flirt at will once he has hardened himself to endure the woman's faithlessness. The same broad pattern appears several times, for instance in Elegy III, 'Change', and in 'Communitie'. In 'The Indifferent' he makes Venus say

> Poore Heretiques in love there bee,
> Which thinke to stablish dangerous constancie.
> But I have told them, since you will be true,
> You shall be true to them, who'are false to you.

In 'The Blossome' his own divided mind is reflected by the division of heart from body and he turns defiantly to the satisfaction of sexual appetite when he is baulked of love. That poem also illustrates Donne's resentment at the fact that the woman may reject him at the level of affectionate love although she has sexual appetite:

> How shall shee know my heart; or having none,
>   Know thee for one?
> Practise may make her know some other part,
> But take my word, shee doth not know a Heart.

His failing of secure satisfaction in love is understandable in the light of his own statement of not knowing what he wanted of women, another frequent topic of the early poetry. This is the theme, phrased in light-hearted rhythms and yet with some seriousness, of 'Negative Love', in which he denies wanting of women what other men want and says he has no idea what it is that he loves, not physical beauty nor virtue nor the mind. In 'The Primrose' he merely argues himself into accepting woman as she is, after the early suggestion of conflict in

> I walke to finde a true Love; and I see
> That 'tis not a mere woman, that is shee,
> But must, or more, or lesse than woman bee.

In 'The Relique', describing 'What miracles wee harmlesse lovers wrought', he says

> First, we lov'd well and faithfully,
> Yet knew not what wee lov'd, nor why,
> Difference of sex no more wee knew,
> Than our Guardian Angells doe.

But, as much of the poetry makes evident, this kind of love was notably incomplete for Donne. He persuades himself of having reached a solution of the conflict in 'The Extasie':

> This Extasie doth unperplex
>   (We said) and tell us what we love,
> Wee see by this, it was not sexe,
>   Wee see, we saw not what did move.

And what we want of love, he goes on to suggest, is a guarantee of union that will give an assured defence against isolation:

> When love, with one another so
>   Interinanimates two soules,

> That abler soule, which thence doth flow,
>> Defects of loneliness controules.
> Wee then, who are this new soule, know,
>> Of what we are compos'd, and made,
> For, th'Atomies of which we grow,
>> Are soules, whom no change can invade.

Once able to feel this assurance of unfailing companion-ship he can turn to the satisfaction of physical appetite, treating this as a means by which the other union can give itself tangible expression:

> So must pure lovers soules descend
>> T'affections, and to faculties,
> Which sense may reach and apprehend,
>> Else a great Prince in prison lies.

*   *   *   *   *

The complexity of Donne's feelings about affection and physical appetite is due in part to his preoccupation with bodily decay and death. The strength and persistence of the preoccupation hardly need illustration; they appear in poems, in the 'Biathanatos', in sermons, and in the final gesture in his last illness of being painted in a shroud and keeping the painting by him as he died. The compulsive quality of the preoccupation is effectively demonstrated in 'The Autumnal', in which he made a notable effort to achieve a calmer view of old age. Addressed to his elderly patroness, Mrs Herbert, it celebrates for about thirty-six lines the quiet autumnal beauty of her face; and then suddenly, with the intellectual gusto that often seems in Donne an index of emotional pressure below, he takes a compulsive glance at the slightly later phase, the 'Winter-faces'

> Whose *Eyes* seeke light within, for all here's shade;
>> Whose *mouthes* are holes, rather worne out, than made;

Whose every tooth to a severall place is gone,
  To vexe their soules at *Resurrection*;
  Name not these living *Deaths-heads* unto mee,
  For these, not *Ancient*, but *Antique* be.

Since it was to this that Mrs Herbert must approximate if
she had the good fortune to live a little longer, Donne had
to find a turn of thought that would lead him back to
politer reflections. He does it abruptly and with a weakness in the structure of his thought that reveals the disturbing intrusiveness of the previous lines:

I hate extreames; yet I had rather stay
  With *Tombs*, than *Cradles*, to weare out a day.

His preoccupation with the theme suggests that death
was ambivalent to him (and we know from 'Biathanatos'
that it was), but with his vigour of mind there is none of
the usual easy welcoming of death as a rest or a release,
not even when he was desperately ill. Dying is a living
experience, one that he prepares for strenuously, and he
struggles endlessly against the fear that afterwards there
is nothing but the repose of annihilation and final disintegration. Some of the most forcefully written lines of
'The Second Anniversary' are those given up to the 'Contemplation of our state in our death-bed', where all the
experiences of dying, besides the rotting of the body, the
anticipated worms and the burial, are gone over in advance
with that same effect of mentally heightening the experience as the Epithalamions achieved for sexual union. In
the anticipation of death he feels fear and not longing, but
the constant effort of the religious writings is to convert
the fear to longing:

This consolation from the Holy Ghost makes my mid-night
noone, mine Executioner a Physitian. . . . It makes my death-
bed, a mariage-bed, And my Passing-Bell, an Epithalamion.
(Sermon at St Paul's, Whitsunday, 1625.)

24

The effort of anticipation directed towards death is a way of bracing himself to meet what he recoils from but knows must come. Donne's preoccupation with death appears to be connected with his sense of disillusionment in the experiences of life. It seems to be generally true that we shrink from the successive phases of life, with their changing pattern of possibilities and limitations, in proportion as we feel that we are not getting all we should from the earlier phases. Donne's great courage and intellectual robustness appear in his determination not to hide from himself the necessity of meeting those phases of experience that he knows lie ahead of him. But because of the underlying reluctance he forces himself to go forward to meet them before they are due:

> Sweetest love, I do not goe,
> For wearinesse of thee,
> Nor in hope the world can show
> A fitter Love for mee;
> But since that I
> Must dye at last, 'tis best,
> To use my selfe in jest
> Thus by fain'd deaths to dye.

Bodily decay and death are the most dramatic events that he feels compelled to foreknow, but the same tendency appears in other contexts. It shows itself in 'Loves Usury', an early poem that illustrates in brief compass several of Donne's significant preoccupations. It offers a bargain with love, by which for every hour of carefree and affection-free sexual adventuring that Donne can enjoy in his youth, he will submit in middle-age to twenty hours of being really in love. The poem indicates that he recognized intellectually, before he was ready to welcome it, the coming of a new phase in which mutual affections would entangle him with a woman, and even the attempt at affectionless sexuality would be a thing of the past. The possibility that besides his loving her she may love him strikes him as the worst of the entanglement:

> Doe thy will then, then subject and degree,
> And fruit of love, Love I submit to thee,
> Spare mee till then, I'll beare it, though she bee
> One that loves mee.

The poem describes exactly what happened, though in fact Donne fell in love with Anne More and stopped philandering before he was thirty. It illustrates his tendency to go forward in thought to a phase of life that had not yet arrived for him.

Besides concern with the entanglements of affection, 'Loves Usury' also deals with the contrast between affection and the simple enjoyment of bodily pleasure. One is reminded of the recurrent theme in the early poems of the relative importance of the lovers' bodies and their souls, or minds, of which the significant feature seems to be the capacity for affection. The fact of the body with its possibility of decay is ambivalent to him: at one time the soul, 'whom no change can invade', seems all-important, but at other times the spiritual necessity of the body seems compelling, as it continues to seem, even in the period of the Sermons:

> We begin with this; That the Kingdom of Heaven hath not all that it must have to consummate perfection, till it have bodies too. In those infinite millions of millions of generations, in which the holy, blessed, and glorious Trinity enjoyed themselves one another, and no more, they thought not their glory so perfect, but that it might receive an addition from creatures; and therefore they made a world, a material world, a corporeall world, they would have bodies. (8 March 1621)

The affection and companionship he valued were for him linked closely with the body (as 'The Extasie' indicates), and consequently he needed reassurance against the fear that all claim on love was forfeited with the decay

of the body. The intention of 'The Autumnal' is to assure
Mrs Herbert of her continued worthiness to be loved, her
acceptability, in spite of the physical changes brought by
age. The same concern appears in a much earlier poem,
Elegy V, 'His Picture'. Here, in his twenties, going on a
journey abroad (said perhaps to have been the expedition
of Essex to Cadiz), he anticipates the most extravagant
physical ravages and sees himself returning emaciated,
generally battered, and his hair white with care; and the
substance of the poem is his effort to reassure himself that
in spite of these ravages he will still be worth loving.

Affection and the body are linked in yet another way,
in that he sees affection as a guarantee against the bodily
disintegration that he so much dreaded. The fantasy of
someone else's love serving to reunite his disintegrating
body appears, for instance, in 'A Valediction: of my name,
in the window':

> Or thinke this ragged bony name to bee
> My ruinous Anatomie.
>
> Then, as all my soules bee,
> Emparadis'd in you, (in whom alone
>   I understand, and grow and see,)
>   The rafters of my body, bone
> Being still with you, the Muscle, Sinew, and Veine,
>   Which tile this house, will come againe.
>
> Till my returne, repaire
> And recompact my scattered body so.

Much the same fantasy of the power of love to maintain
the integration of the body appears in 'The Funerall',
where he asks for 'That subtile wreath of haire, which
crowns my arme' to be buried with him,

> For 'tis my outward Soule,
> Viceroy to that, which then to heaven being gone,

Will leave this to controule,
And keep these limbes, her Provinces, from dissolution.

For if the sinewie thread my braine lets fall
    Through every part,
Can tye those parts, and make mee one of all;
These haires which upward grew, and strength and art
    Have from a better braine,
Can better do'it . . .

Later in his life, of course, it was the love of God that was
to prevent his final bodily disintegration:

To save this body from the condemnation of everlasting cor-
ruption, where the wormes that we breed are our betters, because
they have a life, where the dust of dead Kings is blowne into the
street, and the dust of the street blowne into the River, and the
muddy River tumbled into the Sea, and the Sea remaunded into
all the veynes and channels of the earth; to save this body from
everlasting dissolution, dispersion, dissipation, and to make it in
a glorious Resurrection, not onely a Temple of the holy Ghost,
but a Companion of the holy Ghost in the kingdome of heaven,
this *Christ* became this *Jesus*. (Lincoln's Inn, Sunday after
Trinity, 1621)

It seems clear enough that in some Renaissance moods
the demonstrable death of the body was a more compelling
thought, needing fewer reminders from piety or prudence,
than the survival of the soul. The two, in fact, were not
easily held apart in thought; the fusion shows, for instance, in *Measure for Measure* in the concentrated incon-
sistency of Claudio's two horrors:

Ay, but to die, and go we know not where;
To lie in cold obstruction, and to rot.

Macbeth can be made to tell himself that if there were no
ill consequences of the assassination in this earthly life—
but here upon this bank and shoal of time—'We'd jump
the life to come'. It is the risk, not the certainty of an

after-life that gives Hamlet pause when he thinks of death as a welcome sleep—'perchance to dream'; not the certainty but 'the dread of something after death'. If death as a dreamless sleep could plausibly be presented as a longing of despair it was evidently something that Renaissance man could conceive of and, in a different mood, could fear.

For Donne the nature of the soul was certainly not to be taken for granted, unreflectively. As E. M. Simpson shows (*The Prose Works of John Donne*, Oxford, 1948), he examined the question explicitly, concluding that the soul is not eternal, has not always existed, since God creates it in the very act of infusing it into the body, but affirming his belief that once created it has 'a blessed perpetuity'. Thus he has to believe that although it comes into existence on entering the body it does not cease to exist on going out of it. So long as he could believe in this immortal soul he could confidently believe in God's mercy upon it; Simpson quotes his letter to Sir Henry Goodyer: 'As our soul is infused when it is created, and created when it is infused, so at her going out, Gods mercy is had by asking, and that is asked by having.'

But for mercy to be possible, belief in the soul's immortality is crucial. It is to this belief at the moment of death that Donne seems to refer in the last stanza of 'A Hymne to God the Father'. In the first two stanzas he anticipates, confidently if humbly, forgiveness of his share of original sin, his recurrent sins, the sins into which he has led others, and the sins of early life, shunned now 'a yeare, or two: but wallowed in, a score'. In other words, he considers everything that might lead to damnation and affirms his faith in God's forgiveness. But yet something prevents God from 'having' Donne:

> When thou hast done, thou hast not done,
> For I have more.

I have a sinne of feare, that when I have spunne
   My last thred, I shall perish on the shore;
Sweare by thy selfe, that at my death thy sonne
   Shall shine as he shines now, and heretofore;
And, having done that, Thou hast done,
     I feare no more.

'To perish' means for Donne at times 'to be damned' but at others 'to cease to exist' (as when he says 'every compounded thing may perish'). The fact that the stanza could sound—perhaps even to Donne himself—as if it referred to the fear of damnation made it less unsuitable for devotional purposes, but its literal statement of a fear of extinction has too rich a context in Donne's earlier poems and the feeling of the age to be brushed aside as an accident of wording. If it is taken (as by Simpson) to express simply a fear of damnation the point of the poem is lost, for its whole structure consists in the affirmation of the first two stanzas that he is not damned but forgiven, followed by the confession that even so he has yet another fear.

This was the last of his long anticipations, the culmination of his search for the protracted moment and the arrest of time and change. With Donne's capacity for disillusionment, and his sense, conveyed so vividly in 'An Anatomie of the World', of the loss of a golden age, it was only strenuously and in defiance of fear that he could assure himself of possessing an unshakeable faith in a blessed perpetuity.

2

Experience and Symbol in Blake

ONE of the difficulties in coming to Blake's poetry is to know where to focus attention. So formidable a mass of exegesis and comment has accumulated during the last generation, and some of it so little less obscure than what the poet himself wrote, that on first approaching the poetry (or returning to it after a nonage acquaintance) the reader is liable to feel baffled. If we read only those short poems that seem fairly comprehensible, we may lose much of their meaning by ignoring their relation to the obviously esoteric writings, and if we struggle with the 'prophetic books' and the commentators' quasi-religious exegesis, we may well miss the distinctive enjoyment of Blake as a poet. How far to follow the journeyings of the commentators as they get more and more distant from the poem Blake wrote is a central problem for literary criticism. For those who could read there was an impressive and valuable quality in the poems long before their esoteric meanings were taken seriously. *The Tyger* was widely popular even among Blake's contemporaries in eighteenth-century London. Later on, Edward FitzGerald, Rossetti, and Swinburne were all responsive to the quality of his work as soon as they met it. An appreciation of Blake's power as an English poet, not as a preserve for initiates, must remain the nucleus to which we assimilate more or less of the remoter significance that his writing can be shown to possess.

The remoter significance has been studied—if not exhaustively, for the elaborations it invites seem inexhaustible—at least at stupefying length. An array of books devoted to his moral, religious, and political doctrines testify to the profound importance of the topics that exercised Blake and to the power and suggestiveness of a symbolic treatment that still fascinates good minds and seems worth struggling to comprehend. Yet the need for all this exegesis, its own obscurity, and the divergent views of different commentators point to the disturbing feature of Blake's writing: his failure to achieve sufficient control of his readers' response, even the response of those particularly well equipped for reading him.

The Tyger serves as well as any poem to illustrate the problem of drawing the line between critical elucidation and doctrinal exegesis:

> Tyger! Tyger! burning bright
> In the forests of the night,
> What immortal hand or eye
> Could frame thy fearful symmetry?
>
> In what distant deeps or skies
> Burnt the fire of thine eyes?
> On what wings dare he aspire?
> What the hand dare seize the fire?
>
> And what shoulder, & what art,
> Could twist the sinews of thy heart?
> And when thy heart began to beat,
> What dread hand? & what dread feet?
>
> What the hammer? what the chain?
> In what furnace was thy brain?
> What the anvil? what dread grasp
> Dare its deadly terrors clasp?
>
> When the stars threw down their spears,
> And water'd heaven with their tears,
> Did he smile his work to see?
> Did he who made the Lamb make thee?

> Tyger! Tyger! burning bright
> In the forests of the night,
> What immortal hand or eye,
> Dare frame thy fearful symmetry?

At simplest reading the poem is a contemplation of the fact that, besides peacefulness and gentleness, the world includes fierce strength terrifying in its possibilities of destructiveness but also impressive and admirable, a stupendous part of creation and seemingly a challenge to the idea of a benign Creator. To see that the tiger's fierceness and the lamb's gentleness are also contrasting qualities of the human mind is a very slight extension beyond the simplest literal sense. The theme is a commonplace, and also a fact of supreme human importance, the focus of sharp psychological conflict in individual minds and of unending theological and philosophical discussion. What Blake's fine poem does, is to let us contemplate the facts in their emotional intensity and conflict, and to share his complex attitude of awe, terror, admiration, near-bafflement, and attempted acceptance.

The commentators' extended but limiting interpretations sacrifice Blake's combination of a very general, complex meaning with a vivid phrase-embodied symbol. It is important for an understanding of Blake as a poet (rather than a teacher in parables) to see that he presents the fierceness of nature not through a symbolic object—'a tiger'—but through that object embodied in particular language. The description 'burning bright', for instance, has important uncertainties of meaning: we may (in view of the second stanza) think primarily of the two burning eyes in the darkness, but the phrase itself makes the whole tiger a symbol of a 'burning' quality—wrath, passion, ardour perhaps; but then again the word 'bright' modifies the kind of burning suggested: it may convey incandescence, white heat, and it brings a sense of light,

33

something glorious and shining in the quality symbolized. The essential thing is to recognize how rich a cluster of half-activated associations and potential feelings and attitudes is stimulated by the symbolic language, and how inadequately it can be expressed through an elaboration of formulated and organized ideas.

Extended interpretation along an ordered line of thought raises doubts and divergences of opinion. Take, for instance, the fifth stanza of *The Tyger*. The words have a wide range of echoes and half allusions in each mind, but the central sense needed for the mere construing of the poem is explicit and unambiguous once we see that the stanza refers to the effect of the tiger's creation. Blake asks, with scarcely believing awe, whether the Creator smiled with satisfaction in what he had made when in fact its ferocious strength was so appalling that even the stars abandoned their armed formidability (the spears suggested by their steely glitter) and broke down in tears.

The commentators, however, each following up the allusions and associations that mean most to him, elaborate far beyond this. Gardner suggests that the stars, symbols of material power, cast aside the instruments of strife and take on pity; and the Creator, now become the God of Innocence, 'smiles upon the triumph of the Lamb'. He amplifies by saying: 'The stanza of the Lamb is the only one in which not only the tyger of wrath and rebellion is brought to harmony, but the universe of stars and night as well. The tyger lies down with the Lamb.' The exegesis of Wicksteed, always honestly explicit, goes farther. He thinks the theme is the Incarnation, the stars symbolizing 'the hard cold realm of Reason and war, that held the earth before Compassion came with Christ'. At the end of his long commentary, after the convincing suggestion that the tiger is nothing less indeed than the Divine spark, the fiercely struggling individuality . . .', he concludes,

34

'And yet when we ask ourselves, Is it good to be alive and to burn with quenchless desire, with love half-realized and with purpose ever imperfectly fulfilled? the incarnate heart of Deity in ourselves responds, with the smile of daybreak, that the spirits which discern and divide and contend in labour and agony, are but glimpses of the Great Light that shall unite and heal in strength and tenderness and joy.'

The objections to this kind of writing as comment on Blake are first that it imports into the poem intellectual meanings that are too remotely and indirectly derived from the words, if they can claim to derive from them at all, and second that the parish-magazine quality of sentiment it expresses is totally foreign to the tautness and strength of mind Blake invites us to share.

Yet it would be a worse mistake to ignore the deep seriousness of Blake's preoccupations and his constant concern with fundamental questions of human life. This quality of his work is put beyond doubt by any responsive reading of the symbolic books; and even an inkling of what he was attempting there reflects back on our reading of the shorter poems, not mainly in throwing light on particular symbols but in putting beyond question the spirit in which he approached poetry. It is obvious that for Blake any separation of art from moral problems and belief would have seemed ridiculous; the understanding and evaluation of human experience, especially in certain crucial situations, was his constant object in writing.

The short poems as a whole are finer than the long books as a whole, not only for their more secure control of the reader's response (their 'better communication' if we care to use that uncertain term), but for their more direct statement of human experience in place of the too-cosmic or cosmologized disguise of experience in the books. They include some in which Blake makes a direct moral comment on the London world of his time, using his simple metres to give force and emphasis, as in the *Holy Thursday* of *Songs of Experience* (1794):

> Is this a holy thing to see
> In a rich and fruitful land,
> Babes reduc'd to misery,
> Fed with cold and usurous hand?
>
> Is that trembling cry a song?
> Can it be a song of joy?
> And so many children poor?
> It is a land of poverty!

More usually, however, Blake is wrestling with the psychological and moral problems of us all, those that are inescapable in family life and in the contact of old with young and men with women. These problems and their effects on our personality are the ultimate material of the symbolic books, too, but in the short poems they receive clearer statement. *Infant Sorrow* imagines the protest of the child at birth, its first experience of danger and constraint, its rage and its reluctant submission:

> My mother groan'd! my father wept.
> Into the dangerous world I leapt:
> Helpless, naked, piping loud:
> Like a fiend hid in a cloud.
>
> Struggling in my father's hands,
> Striving against my swadling bands,
> Bound and weary I thought best
> To sulk upon my mother's breast.

For Blake, the father (and any God in which he saw the image of the father) was a figure of oppression and jealousy, and the mother was obliged to join the father in his terrified and tyrannous control of the child. So in *The Book of Urizen* (1794), when Enitharmon has borne the child Orc to Los:

> They took Orc to the top of a mountain.
> O how Enitharmon wept!
> They chain'd his young limbs to the rock
> With the Chain of Jealousy
> Beneath Urizen's deathful shadow.

The perpetual cycle of conflict thus initiated between young and old is expressed in the dream-like poem *The Mental Traveller*, which also illustrates his sense of the conflict and mutual exploitation in sexual attraction, a theme expressed simply in *The Golden Net* and in subtler forms recurrently throughout his work.

In Blake's eyes the possessiveness of sexual love and the constraint exercised by the old each contributed to the creation of an abstract moral code, and with it a sense of guilt. Contrasted with all that these things implied, he kept in mind the state of Innocence, the 'contrary state of the human soul', and throughout his work he was exploring the relation between the perfect possibilities he felt in human life and the lamentable confusions and imperfections that appear in actual experience. Faced with the sources of conflict and sin in his own personality, he dealt with the problem of guilt by developing his conviction that there is nothing to be afraid of in human personality.

> Mutual Forgiveness of each Vice,
> Such are the gates of Paradise,

he wrote in denouncing the abstract Commandments, and asserted in *The Marriage of Heaven and Hell* (*c*. 1793) that 'The road of excess leads to the palace of wisdom'. In *The Book of Los* the introductory stanzas put forward the same ideas in describing the condition of innocence:

'O Times remote!
'When Love & Joy were adoration,
'And none impure were deem'd:
'Not Eyeless Covet,
'Nor Thin-lip'd Envy,
'Nor Bristled Wrath,
'Nor Curled Wantonness.

'But Covet was poured full,
'Envy fed with fat of lambs,
'Wrath with lion's gore,
'Wantonness lull'd to sleep
'With the virgin's lute
'Or sated with her love:

'Till Covet broke his locks & bars
'And slept with open doors;
'Envy sung at the rich man's feast;
'Wrath was follow'd up and down
'By a little ewe lamb,
'And Wantonness on his own true love
'Begot a giant race.'

It was out of these basic problems and attitudes that Blake built his moral and quasi-religious system, and it was in the attempt to express adequately the complexity revealed in an extended and subtle exploration of them that he developed his intricate mythologies.

But neither vast mythopoeic cosmologies nor brief and clear-sighted statements of basic psychological problems could by themselves have given him any importance as a poet. For that his extraordinarily fine handling of language was needed. His rhythms deserve more attention than the length of this essay permits. In his best work they are at the same time forceful and supple, some based on ballad metres, some metrically free and influenced by the Bible, but all returning again and again to the rhythm of speech.

Notice the style of folk rhyme and incantation ('Double, double toil and trouble') in Blake's poem about being dogged by his 'Spectre':

> He scents thy footsteps in the snow,
> Wheresoever thou dost go
> Thro' the wintry hail & rain.
> When wilt thou return again?

And in the later stanzas of the poem observe the supple variety in what is deliberately repetitive and might have become tum-ti-tum:

> Seven more loves weep night & day
> Round the tombs where my loves lay,
> And seven more loves attend each night
> Around my couch with torches bright.
>
> And seven more Loves in my bed
> Crown with vine my mournful head,
> Pitying & forgiving all
> My transgression, great & small.

In the short poems an outstanding quality is the immense compression of meaning, sometimes of a simple kind—as in 'Old Nobodaddy' for the God of the churches, or the 'Marriage hearse' of *London*—and sometimes far more complex. A closely related feature of his writing, often a means of compression and notably contrasting with the contemporary practice of his time, was the trust with which he launched himself into imagery and ideas that carried symbolic implications scarcely susceptible of reasoned exposition, and that gained their coherence and ordered effect through unexplicit associations and incompletely formulated reference:

> Never seek to tell thy love
> Love that never told can be:
> For the gentle wind does move
> Silently, invisibly.

39

I told my love, I told my love,
I told her all my heart,
Trembling, cold, in ghastly fears—
Ah, she doth depart.

Soon as she was gone from me
A traveller came by
Silently, invisibly—
He took her with a sigh.

The suggestions are of something too terrifying in the ultimate nature of love to be disclosed, of the man's need nevertheless to try to establish full knowledge between them, of the woman not able to bear it, lost to him and taken by some invisible agency that moves gently, perhaps regretfully, but irrevocably. The 'traveller' who takes her may carry echoes of 'time' and 'death', but all we know is that when the man tries to break down the conventional limits of the communicable some silent, invisible agency comes into action, ends their union, and puts the woman beyond his reach. We could go on to speculate that the silent, invisible traveller might be just some aspect of fear-inducing conventionality, for Blake's lines to the God of the churches refer to the same characteristics:

Why art thou silent & invisible,
Father of Jealousy?

There is the obvious psycho-analytic interpretation in terms of the oedipal situation, and among the commentators Wicksteed and Gardner offer yet other views, both plausible and each different. The fact seems to be that these speculative 'meanings' all isolate one or two harmonics from the note. Left to itself the poem half evokes these and probably many other ideas; repeated listening, with strict moderation in the use of intellectual ingenuities, seems the likeliest way of getting from the words something of the effect that led Blake to find them satisfying.

The risks in such an approach to obscure poetry are clearly evident, especially the risks of wasting time on the charlatans of emotion and incantation. But unless we take them we shall miss the enjoyment of poems whose obscurity, in T. S. Eliot's words,[1] 'is due to the suppression of "links in the chain", or explanatory and connecting matter, and not to incoherence, or to the love of cryptogram'. 'Such selection of a sequence of images and ideas', he continues, 'has nothing chaotic about it. There is a logic of the imagination as well as a logic of concepts.'

Blake can be seen suppressing expository links in a simple way in *The Tyger*. The exclamation now on its own as the end of a stanza—

> And when thy heart began to beat
> What dread hand & what dread feet

—was in the early draft the opening of a sentence that went on:

> Could fetch it from the furnace deep
> And in thy horrid ribs dare steep
> In the well of sanguine woe?

As Blake revised, the broken sentence seemed to convey the meaning far enough, besides preserving the full exclamatory force.

A more complex and extremely fine example of his method is provided by the 'Introduction' to *Songs of Experience* and *Earth's Answer* which follows it. Certain familiar themes are used, their ordinary associations recalled but unexpectedly modified, and they are set in relation—but not an explicitly defined relation—to totally

---

[1] Preface to T. S. Eliot's translation of St-J. Perse's *Anabasis* (London, 1930).

41

different and unfamiliar ideas. The 'Introduction' might
seem at first glance a straightforward treatment of the
Fall, with its reference to

> The Holy Word
> That walk'd among the ancient trees,

> Calling the lapsed Soul,
> And weeping in the evening dew:
> That might controll
> The starry pole,
> And fallen, fallen light renew!

Even here the word 'ancient' for the trees unexpectedly
modifies the ordinary notion of Eden; it is taken up again
in *Earth's Answer* when, in denouncing the jealous, love-
chaining God, Earth calls him 'the father of the ancient
men'. The 'weeping' is given an implication of helplessness by the next two stanzas of the 'Introduction' in
which the Holy Word is shown as pleading with Earth,
in effect wooing her to come to him in the permitted
period of darkness:

> 'Turn away no more;
> 'Why wilt thou turn away?
> 'The starry floor,
> 'The wat'ry shore,
> 'Is giv'n thee till the break of day.'

With this helplessness is contrasted the power of the
Creator to reverse, if he would, the darkness of the Fall,

> And fallen, fallen light renew!

The effect is already to convey not only the usual sense of
boundless loss and the grief of the Creator, but with it an
astringent hint of something questionable in the power of
renewal not exercised. Moreover, the lapsed soul is not
man but 'Earth'. In *Earth's Answer* it becomes clear that

Earth is feminine and is being wooed for her love, including her sexual love. The Holy Word has now become

> 'Selfish father of men!
> 'Cruel, jealous, selfish fear!'

And the denunciation of his imprisoning jealousy is combined with Blake's hatred of the conventional restriction of sexual activity to darkness, with its implications of shame and secrecy:

> 'Can delight,
> 'Chain'd in night,
> 'The virgins of youth and morning bear?
>
> 'Does spring hide its joy
> 'When buds and blossoms grow?
> 'Does the sower
> 'Sow by night,
> 'Or the plowman in darkness plow?'

The fallen light of the 'Introduction' thus gathers a further meaning. Behind the two poems, moreover, there lurks the idea which Blake developed in the prophetic books that the Creation was a division in God and itself constituted the Fall:

> Six days they shrunk up from existence,
> And on the seventh day they rested,
> And they bless'd the seventh day, in sick hope,
> And forgot their eternal life.
>
> (*The Book of Urizen*, IX, 17-20)

But that is not made explicit here, and the exegesis is perhaps not needed. What the two poems offer is an unexpected handling of the Fall, with its sexual aspects, in a way that links God's relation to the world with that of men to women, associates the Creator with the jealous patriarch and with the selfish fear in us all, and at the same time shows him helplessly defeated by the refusal of his

creation to submit to jealous control and accept atonement on his terms. The themes are brought together,
with vistas of association down any of which we can pause
and look, rather in the manner of a photomontage. They
are not fully displayed, not explicitly related to one
another, but, although possibly mystifying at first, the
effect is of a pattern that has emotional coherence in spite
of being so remote from discursive logic.

Nevertheless it must be added that the proper pleasure
of the poem is not to be gained by uncomprehending
submission to it as a mysteriously stirring incantation; it
calls for an accurate grasp of the sense of its statements
with the feelings and attitudes they convey; and a developing appreciation involves extended insight into the re-
latedness of themes that may at first seem to be merely
juxtaposed.

Even a brief discussion of Blake's use of language
brings up the nature of his ideas. To balance what was
said before, no skills and subtleties in the handling of
language would have given him much importance as a
poet if it were not for the significance of the concerns that
held him and the worth of his insights and evaluations.
And these cannot be assessed without some attention to
the symbolic aspects of his writing.

The purposes that symbolism served for Blake can best
be seen by considering first the so-called Rossetti manuscript.[1]

From the manuscript book it can be seen that Blake's
poems of this period were personal documents in which
he expressed and tried to come to terms with his own
psychological problems and foci of intense emotion. The
nature of the poems and their sequence are what would be
expected when a writer of genius used a verse form for
self-analysis. At some points the topic he handles is dealt

---

[1] Reproduced, with a commentary, by Wicksteed.

with compactly and completely enough, and in symbols near enough to public intelligibility to create a publishable poem; from poems of this sort he selected *Songs of Experience* for engraving. At other points in the manuscript, what he wrote reflects more fragmentary and shifting states of mind, often expressed incompletely and in symbols too uncertain or unprofitably ambiguous for publication. Something like free association is evident at times, as in poems XV and XVI of the manuscript[1]: the first is an obscure four lines beginning, 'O lapwing thou fliest around the heath', and the second switches to 'Thou hast a lap full of seed'.

Such a flow of important and less-important material is nowadays familiar enough in psycho-analysis; the symbolism thrown up in dreams, waking fantasy, and free association has sometimes to be guessed at, sometimes serves mainly as a bridge from one important topic to another, and only occasionally offers an effective and tolerably certain statement of an important theme. Commentators on Blake, whether wittingly or not, have adopted very much the psycho-analytic method in interpreting further and further the possible implications of phrases, associations, and symbols. They may use the traditional symbolic meaning attached to an idea or they may concentrate on Blake's private symbolism, and they illuminate one passage by reference to similar words or images in another part of his work. In the attempt to understand the long symbolic writings (the so-called prophetic books) this recondite interpretative analysis is carried to extreme lengths.

In these books, Blake's communing with himself about problems of his own personality, seen in manageable form in the Rossetti manuscript, now appears on a vaster

[1] Geoffrey Keynes (Ed.), *Poetry and Prose of William Blake* (London, 1927), p. 92

45

literary scale. When he reached some definite standpoint on a problem, he expounded it in the spirit of a religious teacher and in language clear enough, as for instance when he teaches forgiveness in *The Ghost of Abel* (1822). But this is uncharacteristic; most of the writings reflect his struggles to establish order among apparently conflicting aspects of his own personality expressed as symbolic figures and situations. The uncertainties and conflicts play as big a part as the ordering he achieves, and he sometimes gives the impression not of reporting the resolution of conflicts previously examined but of discovering and threshing out his problems in the process of writing. The personal issues with which he wrestled seemed to him to be also the salient problems of human life. They included questions of the proper place of intellectual control in the total economy of the personality, the place of impulse, the relations between authority and those it controls (and therefore between elders and children), the relations of the sexes, the folly of moral generalities (one law for the lion and the ox), the poison of jealousy, and the overwhelming importance of forgiveness.

The parallel between the prophetic books and Blake's struggle to understand and harmonize features of his own personality is illustrated from the letter to Hayley of 23 October 1804, quoted by Sloss and Wallis and compared with passages of *Jerusalem* and *The Four Zoas*. To Hayley he exclaimed:

> O Glory! and O Delight! I have entirely reduced that spectrous fiend to his station, whose annoyance has been the ruin of my labours for the last passed twenty years of my life. He is the enemy of conjugal love, and is the Jupiter of the Greeks, an iron-hearted tyrant, the ruiner of ancient Greece. . . . Oh! the distress I have undergone, and my poor wife with me; incessantly labouring and incessantly spoiling what I had done well. . . . I thank God with entire confidence that it shall be so no longer—

he is become my servant who domineered over me; he is even as a brother who was my enemy.'

Sloss and Wallis compare this with *The Four Zoas*, VII, 335 ff.:

> Los embrac'd the Spectre, first as a brother,
> Then as another Self, astonish'd, humanizing & in tears,
> In Self-abasement Giving up his Domineering lust.

> 'Thou never canst embrace sweet Enitharmon, terrible Demon, Till
> 'Thou art united with thy Spectre, Consummating by pains & labours
> 'That mortal body, & by Self annihilation back returning
> 'To Life Eternal. . . .'

Other passages in *The Four Zoas* and the opening pages of *Jerusalem* refer to the same struggle with the 'Spectre' (by which Blake seems to have meant something like dependence upon abstract, analytic reasoning). Uncertain as the dating of the later writings must be (owing to Blake's protracted revisions), it seems clear that *The Four Zoas*, at least, was written before the ecstatic letter to Hayley, and it therefore looks as if the illumination he celebrates in that letter occurred after he had been struggling with the problem for a considerable time in the symbolic writings. The likehood that they were not *records* of psychological struggles but to a great extent the form in which the struggles found expression while they actually occurred helps to explain their obscurity and inconsistencies.

An early and unfinished symbolic book, *Tiriel* (c. 1789), shows that there were interesting possibilities in this self-exploratory writing, and that outlandish names and a privately concocted mythology need not have been insuperable barriers to communication. Whatever its inadequacies, *Tiriel* is successful in conveying promptly, and without the need for a wide search through this and other poems, the essential features of its persons and situations: Tiriel, the tyrant father facing death, the sons and daughters reduced by his treatment to futile hatred of him, an alternative form of age in Har and Heva with their childish abdication of any attempt at self-responsibility and control of others, the creature Ijim of tremendous animal vitality confused by the dissemblings and mental complications of Tiriel and his offspring, the witless Zazel reduced to menial tasks and servitude by his cunning brother Tiriel. The poem indicates the promise of the method Blake was experimenting with. It gives him people who are 'real' enough to have intense feelings; they represent figures of family life of deep psychological importance; and at the same time they are hinted at as aspects of every personality, or possibilities of personality development, each with plausible justifications for itself while being in violent conflict with the others. Though Blake reaches no solution, he expresses in more or less dramatic form the diverse qualities and aspects of personality and the situations of conflict in which they meet, and he conveys his sense of the vast importance, the violence, and the confusedness of their struggles.

The nature of the failure met with in the later books is also forecast in *Tiriel*. The persons and action hover uncertainly between intellectually controlled allegory on the one hand, and on the other the representation of concrete situations taken seriously in their own dramatic right but with overtones of symbolic meaning to enrich them; the poem is neither a deliberated allegory like *The Faery Queen*, nor a plunge into the emotional reality of a symbol-charged incident such as *The Ancient Mariner* takes. In the more massive books the same ingredients appear, but the allegory becomes increasingly obscure and the figures and incidents less immediately significant.

Personae and places are introduced abruptly, without sufficient context to establish their meaning and feeling-quality; and the commentators are therefore sent searching through the rest of Blake's writings for a clue to the cipher he is using. Instead of reading a poem in his own language the reader finds himself studying a cabbala, and the rewards he meets will be, in the main, not the rewards of poetry. A passage from *Jerusalem* will illustrate the division of aim between poetry and doctrine, the fumbling between cipher and symbol:

> And Los beheld his Sons and he beheld his Daughters,
> Every one a translucent Wonder, a Universe within,
> Increasing inwards into length, and breadth, and heighth,
> Starry & glorious: and they, every one in their bright loins,
> Have a beautiful golden gate which opens into the vegetative world;
> And every one a gate of rubies & all sorts of precious stones
> In their translucent hearts, which opens into the vegetative world;
> And every one a gate of iron dreadful and wonderful
> In their translucent heads, which opens into the vegetative world.
> And every one had the three regions Childhood, Manhood, & Age.
> But the gate of the tongue, the western gate, in them is clos'd,
> Having a wall builded against it: and thereby the gates
> Eastward & Southward & Northward are incircled with flaming fires.
> And the North is Breadth, the South is Heighth & Depth,
> The East is Inwards, & the West is Outwards every way.
>
> And Los beheld the mild Emanation Jerusalem eastward bending
> Her revolutions toward the Starry Wheels in maternal anguish,
> Like a pale cloud arising from the arms of Beulah's Daughters,
> In Entuthon Benython's deep Vales beneath Golgonooza.

(1)

49

The failure—in large part—of the prophetic writings is not due to the method of allegory or even to the inconsistencies in the cipher, but to Blake's failure in embodiment. A repeated decoding, deliberated and often needing the aid of an external key, has to take the place of an immediate conviction of meaning and feeling. And when Blake takes existing names—London, Highgate, Conway, Albion, etc.—and puts them to his private allegorical purposes, we are worse baffled, since we now have to undo the ordinary associations before trying to tack on his.

Doubtful as must be the rewards of wrestling with the long symbolic books, it would still be a loss not to know some of the passages in which states of mind and dramatic situations are given expression of a fully intelligible and effective kind, even while the symbolic scaffolding around them is baffling. Unexpectedly, too, the verse of the long books has a cumulative appeal in spite of so much that repels. Quotation cannot convey that, but something of the variety and effectiveness of the language and rhythms may be indicated. Though the Biblical echoes are prominent in the following passage, for instance, the completely new, individual note (besides a concern with contemporary social fact) is there too:

'Shall not the King call for Famine from the heath,
'Nor the Priest for Pestilence from the fen,
'To restrain, to dismay, to thin
'The inhabitants of mountain and plain,
'In the day of full-feeding prosperity
'And the night of delicious songs?

'Shall not the Councellor throw his curb
'Of Poverty on the laborious,
'To fix the price of labour,
'To invent allegoric riches?

'And the privy admonishers of men
'Call for Fires in the City,
'For heaps of smoking ruins,
'In the night of prosperity & wantonness,

'To turn man from his path,
'To restrain the child from the womb,
'To cut off the bread from the city,
'That the remnant may learn to obey,

'That the pride of the heart may fail,
'That the lust of the eyes may be quench'd,
'That the delicate ear in its infancy
'May be dull'd, and the nostrils clos'd up,
'To teach mortal worms the path
'That leads from the gates of the Grave?'

(*The Song of Los*, Asia, 9-32)

Again, the whole of Enion's lamentation in Night II of *The Four Zoas* is worth reading for the sake of the dramatic rhetoric, whether or not we know what Enion represents, for here Blake's power is unquestionable and we glimpse the possibilities that might have been realized if he could have handled his dramatic themes more lucidly and with more convincing embodiment. The causes of his relative failure in the prophetic books were multiple and can only be guessed at. The influence of *Ossian* may have led him to rely too readily on the acceptability of an outlandish mythology. Boehme and Swedenborg suggested the possibility of new mystical and religious systems, and seemed to sanction extreme obscurity of utterance.

Above all stands the fact of his having had no adequate reading public whose adverse criticism or lack of comprehension he could have taken seriously. His pugnacious attitude to the dimly conventional figures of his time led him to take the line he indicates in a letter to Dr Trusler, whose writings he was asked to illustrate and who objected to the obscurity of the designs. 'You say', writes Blake, 'that I want somebody to Elucidate my Ideas. What is Grand is necessarily obscure to Weak men. That which can be made Explicit to the Idiot is not worth my care. The wisest of the Ancients consider'd what is not too Explicit as the fittest for Instruction, because it rouzes the faculties to act. I name Moses, Solomon, Esop, Homer, Plato.' However, if we sympathize with this line of justification we are checked by a further assertion in the same letter: 'But I am happy to find a Great Majority of Fellow Mortals who can Elucidate My Visions, & Particularly they have been Elucidated by Children, who have taken a greater delight in contemplating my Pictures than I even hoped. Neither Youth nor Childhood is Folly or Incapacity.' Blake, like many who are unappreciated, seems to have been divided between defiant justification of the obscurity of his work and the belief that people of unspoiled intelligence would find none. He wanted to be understood, but not at the cost of trimming down his meaning to the assimilative capacity of conventional minds. The Hayleys, Truslers, and Crabb Robinsons must always set the tone of cultivated society—of which educated mediocrity necessarily forms the greater part— and in the complacent literary culture of his early life Blake could have scarcely a hint of any effective minority of readers who in his own time or later might understand and value his work. The miracle is that he produced such work at all. He represents a tremendous opportunity in English literature that was largely wasted owing to the reading public's restricted capacities for response; and the combination of greatness and failure in his work is a reminder that a literature consists not of writers only but of their readers too.

3

The Theme of
'The Ancient Mariner'

IN *The Road to Xanadu* Livingston Lowes eschews any attempt to interpret Coleridge's work along psychoanalytic lines, and no doubt at the time he wrote (in the early nineteen-twenties) the dangers of amateur psychoanalytic interpretations were more evident than their promise. At the point where he discusses the problem explicitly he shows that Robert Graves' interpretation of 'Kubla Khan', speculative and undisciplined as well as ham-fisted, founders on several errors of biographical fact which better scholarship would have avoided.

The mutual relevance of an author's personal experience and the characteristics of his writing raises questions which fortunately need not be settled as a preliminary to literary studies, even those influenced by psychological thinking. It seems entirely possible, and wise, to distinguish clearly the biographical or clinical study of the author from the literary assessment or elucidation of his writings. Each may sometimes be used to illuminate the other, though the dangers of an over-simplified view of their interrelation are alarming; but if we take the risk we ought to make it perfectly clear whether our purpose is biographical or literary.

If literary, as mine is here, the essential guiding principle is to keep close to the poem (or whatever the form of writing is) and as far as possible use only what it says, either avoiding or using with extreme caution importations from psychological theory and biography. Even the poet's other writings, though they often give useful confirmatory hints for elucidation, must take second place to the particular poem we are reading. That exists in its own right and forms our only necessary datum for literary criticism.

Yet however conscientiously we focus on the literary task we shall not escape psychological questions. Livingston Lowes' own work shows this. Most of his remarkably thorough and skilful work of scholarly detection and tracking is concentrated on the materials from which the poem was made and on the detailed thought processes of association, condensation, changed emphasis and so on that occurred in Coleridge's mind. This itself is one aspect of a psychological, as well as a literary study. But to the further psychological question of the human significance of the action of 'The Ancient Mariner' he gives very cursory attention. He admits that it matters. He quotes Coleridge on the value in poetry of 'the modifying colours of imagination' giving the interest of novelty to 'a known and familiar landscape', and on the decision that in the 'Lyrical Ballads' Coleridge's 'endeavours should be directed to persons and characters supernatural, or at least romantic; yet so as to transfer from our inward nature a human interest and a semblance of truth sufficient to procure for these shadows of imagination that willing suspension of disbelief for the moment which constitutes poetic faith. . . . With this view I wrote the "Ancient Mariner".'

Livingston Lowes comments '. . . if Coleridge's words mean anything, they mean that some interest deeply human, anchored in the familiar frame of things, was fundamental to his plan' and he asks 'Are there truths of "our inward nature" which do, in fact, uphold and cherish, as we read, our sense of actuality in a phantom universe, peopled with the shadows of a dream?'. He discovers what he takes the human action of the poem to be,

and he treats it with a succinctness that makes a remarkable contrast with his lengthy, scholarly ramblings around
the fragments of Coleridge's building material. He writes:

> But the train of cause and consequence is more than a con-
> solidating factor of the poem. It happens to be life, as every
> human being knows it. You do a foolish or an evil deed, and its
> results come home to you. And they are apt to fall on others too.
> You repent, and a load is lifted from your soul. But you have not
> thereby escaped your deed. You attain forgiveness, but cause and
> effect work on unmoved, and life to the end may be a continued
> reaping of the repented deed's results. That is not a system of
> ethics; it is the inexorable law of life, than which nothing is surer
> or more unchanging. There it stands in your experience and
> mine, 'known and familiar' if anything on earth is so.

This summary of the action is not entirely off the
target, but it is far from being a bull's-eye, and by the
standards of comprehensiveness and precision reached in
the less psychological parts of the book it is pitifully
meagre and inaccurate. Take only the obvious points:
repentance without restitution or confession seldom does
in fact lift a load from the soul, and it is certainly not
repentance that relieves the Mariner (he had bitterly re-
pented long before the Albatross fell off); again, although
he attains forgiveness in the formal sense of being shriven,
his later fate makes it evident that he has never forgiven
himself; moreover his later life doesn't consist in reaping
the results of the deed brought about by the continued
working of cause and effect—results of that kind are
strikingly absent—it consists simply in a long-drawn-out
pilgrimage of repentance with recurrent bouts of acute
remembrance and self-reproach.

* * * * *

The human experience on which Coleridge centres
the poem is the depression and the sense of isolation and
worthlessness which the Mariner describes in Part IV.

The suffering he conveys is of a kind which is perhaps not found except in slightly pathological conditions, but which, pathological or not, has been felt by a great many people. He feels isolated to a degree that baffles expression and reduces him to the impotent, repetitive emphasis that becomes doggerel in schoolroom reading:

> Alone, alone, all, all alone,
> Alone on a wide wide sea!

At the same time he is not just physically isolated but is socially abandoned, even by those with the greatest obligations:

> And never a saint took pity on
> My soul in agony.

With this desertion the beauty of the ordinary world has been taken away:

> The many men so beautiful!
> And they all dead did lie . . .

All that is left, and especially, centrally, oneself, is disgustingly worthless:

> And a thousand thousand slimy things
> Lived on; and so did I.

With the sense of worthlessness there is also guilt. When he tried to pray

> A wicked whisper came and made
> My heart as dry as dust.

And enveloping the whole experience is the sense of sapped energy, oppressive weariness:

> For the sky and the sea, and the sea and the sky
> Lay like a load on my weary eye,
> And the dead were at my feet.

This, the central experience, comes almost at the middle of the poem. It is the nadir of depression to which the earlier stanzas sink: the rest of the poem describes what is in part recovery and in part aftermath. You need not have been a spell-bound mariner in a supernatural Pacific in order to have felt this mood. Coleridge knew it well, and 'Dejection' and 'The Pains of Sleep' deal with closely related experiences.

A usual feature of these states of pathological misery is their apparent causelessness. The depression cannot be rationally explained; the conviction of guilt and worthlessness is out of proportion to any ordinary offence actually committed. In the story of 'The Ancient Mariner' Coleridge finds a crime which, in its symbolic implications, is sufficient to merit even his suffering. The Mariner's sin, as many have realized, was that in killing the albatross he rejected a social offering. Why he did so is left quite unexplained. It was a wanton bit of self-sufficiency. It was enough for Coleridge that this was a dreadful thing which one might do, and he did it. The Mariner wantonly obliterated something that loved him and represented in a supernatural way the possibility of affection in the world. The depth of meaning the act held for Coleridge can be gauged from the curious self-exculpation with which he ends 'The Pains of Sleep'. That poem is a fragment of case-history recounting three nights of bad dreams:

> Fantastic passions! maddening brawl!
> And shame and terror over all!
> Deeds to be hid which were not hid,
> Which all confused I could not know
> Whether I suffered, or I did:
> For all seem'd guilt, remorse or woe . . .

Characteristically, he assumes that these sufferings must be a punishment for something or other. Yet by the standards of waking life and reason he feels himself to be innocent. He never explicitly mentions what the supposed offence might be. But the last two lines, in which he protests his innocence, reveal implicitly what crime alone could merit such punishment:

> Such punishments, I said, were due
> To natures deepliest stained with sin . . .
> But wherefore, wherefore fall on me?
> To be beloved is all I need,
> And whom I love, I love indeed.

With those lines in mind we can judge better the force of the stanza in 'The Ancient Mariner':

> The spirit that bideth by himself
> In the land of mist and snow,
> He loved the bird that loved the man
> Who shot him with his bow.

This for Coleridge was the most terrible possibility among the sins. Why, in 'The Pains of Sleep', is he innocent of the fatal sin?—because he aims at nothing beyond affection and union with others, gives no allegiance to more individual interests in the outer world which might flaw his complete devotion. It is only in the light of the last two lines that the introductory section of the poem yields its meaning. Explaining that he is not accustomed to saying formal prayers before going to sleep, Coleridge continues

> But silently, by slow degrees,
> My spirit I to Love compose.
> In humble trust mine eyelids close,
> With reverential resignation . . .

And then one realises that he is protesting against being visited with the horrible dreams *in spite of* cultivating submissive affection and so guarding against the one sin that could merit such punishments.

The Mariner committed the sin. Yet Coleridge knew that by the ordinary standards of the workaday world the act was not, after all, very terrible. Hence the ironic stanzas which show the indifference of the mariners to the real meaning of the deed. At first

> Ah wretch! said they, the bird to slay,
> That made the breeze to blow!

And then,

> 'Twas right, said they, such birds to slay,
> That bring the fog and mist.

It is not by the ordinary standards of social life that the Mariner could be condemned, any more than Coleridge felt he himself could in 'The Pains of Sleep'. We are to take it, I think, though the point is not made explicit, that the Mariner feels horror and guilt immediately on committing the crime; there is no suggestion that its hideousness needs demonstrating to him. His sense of guilt is there from the start. The public condemnation, the curse of his shipmates, is a later and only external confirmation of his sense of being worthless. He is cursed, by them, not for the crime he had committed but for the calamity that his action happens to have produced. The essence of the poem is a private sense of guilt, intense out of all proportion to public rational standards. The supernatural machinery of the poem allowed Coleridge to convey something of this—for the small impulsive act which presses a supernatural trigger does form an effective parallel to the hidden impulse which has such a devastating meaning for one's irrational, and partly unconscious, private standards. It is a fiction that permits the expression of real experience.

The total pattern of experience in 'The Ancient Mariner' includes partial recovery from the worst depression. The offence for which the dejection and isolation were punishment was the wanton rejection of a very simple social union. One step towards recovery is suggested in 'The Pains of Sleep'. It is a return to a submissive sense of childlike weakness and distress:

> O'ercome with sufferings strange and wild,
> I wept as I had been a child;
> And having thus by tears subdued
> My anguish to a milder mood . . .

The Mariner's sufferings have first to reduce him to a dreadful listlessness and apathy. He contrasts his condition then with the calm activity of the Moon going about her ordinary business in the universe, accompanied by the stars which, unlike him, still have their right to be welcomed. He treats them as if they were a secure family, and, significantly, they now fill him with longing—'he yearneth':

> In his loneliness and fixedness he yearneth towards the journeying moon, and the stars that still sojourn, yet still move onward; and everywhere the blue sky belongs to them, and is their appointed rest, and their native country and their own natural homes, which they enter unannounced, as lords that are certainly expected and yet there is a silent joy at their arrival.

He has to reach complete listlessness before there is any chance of recovery. His state at the turning point makes a significant contrast to the desperate activity—the courageous snatching at hope in the direction from which he personally has decided salvation must come—which is suggested earlier by his watch for a sail and his final effort of hope:

> I bit my arm, I sucked the blood,
> And cried, A sail! a sail!

All this directed effort and expense of spirit is futile in the state of mind which Coleridge describes. Only when his individual striving has sunk to a low ebb can the recovery begin.

This naturally gives the impression, characteristic of these states of depression, that the recovery is fortuitous. It comes unpredictably and seemingly from some trivial accident. This part of the psychological experience Coleridge has paralleled in the supernatural machinery of the tale by means of the dicing between Death and Life-in-Death. To the sufferer there seems no good reason why he shouldn't simply die, since he feels that he has thrown up the sponge. Instead, chance has it that he lives on.

The fact of its being Life-in-Death who wins the Mariner shows how incomplete his recovery is going to be. Nevertheless some degree of recovery from the nadir of dejection does unpredictably occur. It begins with the momentary rekindling of simple pleasure in the things around him, at the very moment when he has touched bottom in apathy:

> Oh happy living things! no tongue
> Their beauty might declare . . .

It is the beginning of recovery because what is kindled is a recognition not only of their beauty but also of the worth of their existence and, by implication, of his own. For he had previously associated himself with them—the thousand slimy things—in denying their right to live when the men were dead:

> He despiseth the creatures of the calm. And envieth that they should live and so many lie dead.

The earlier exclamation, in the depths of self-condemnation, 'The many men, so beautiful!' is not one of simple pleasure in the things around him. He is still absorbed in his self-contempt and uses his recognition of other men's beauty only as a further lash against himself. Or, to put it differently, when he was in the depths the only beauty he would consent to see was beauty dead and spoilt; the beauty still present in the world he denied.

The moment when the worst of his load is lifted and the Albatross drops off his neck into the sea is not brought about, as Livingston Lowes would have it, by repentance. Coleridge's account of the state of acute depression, with the sense of guilt and worthlessness, is much more accurate; it emphasises the impression of something fortuitous about the impulse that rises in him and brings him back to life:

> A spring of love gushed from my heart,
> And I blessed them unaware:
> Sure my kind saint took pity on me,
> And I blessed them unaware.

The repetition of 'unaware' stresses the fortuitousness, something paralleled by the fall of the dice on the spectral bark. At this turning point in the Mariner's experience there is an unaccountable renewal of the impulse of love towards other living things. That is enough; responsive life has been waiting around him and the Holy Mother immediately sends the rain and sleep he needs.

In the second stanza of 'Dejection' Coleridge describes a mood in which, like the Mariner, he watches the beauty of natural things but fails in the vital response:

> I see them all so excellently fair,
> I see, not feel, how beautiful they are!

But the Mariner's turning towards partial recovery depends on a mood in which the vital impulse does come. His own impulse saves him, and this is represented as his guardian saint, whereas earlier 'never a saint took pity . . .'. It is now his guardian saint who invokes the angelic spirits to work the ship back to port.

His returning joy in living things comes, of course, from his own changed attitude and his willingness to look

differently on the world. Coleridge made this point also in
'Dejection':

> O Lady! we receive but what we give,
> And in our life alone does nature live . . .
> Ah! from the soul itself must issue forth
> A light, a glory, a fair luminous cloud
> Enveloping the Earth—
> And from the soul itself must there be sent
> A sweet and potent voice, of his own birth,
> Of all sweet sounds the life and element!

From this one turns to 'The Ancient Mariner' at a later
stage in the recovery:

> Around, around, flew each sweet sound,
> Then darted to the Sun;
> Slowly the sounds came back again,
> Now mixed, now one by one.

Still later the band of seraphs who

> stood as signals to the land,
> Each one a lovely light

can be associated with

> A light, a glory, a fair luminous cloud.

Coleridge accepts sound and light and colour as the
simplest adequate expression of the beauty of the world
which ebbed and flowed with his own spirits.

In consistent development of the general theme, the
Mariner's recovery leads on to reunion with the very
simple and humble kinds of social life. He joins the
villagers in the formal expression of atonement with each
other, and with the source of love, which he sees in their
religious worship. But it would be a mistake to think of
this as anything like full recovery. For one thing he never
again belongs to a settled community, but has to pass

from land to land. For another thing there is the periodic 'abreaction' and confession that he has to resort to:

> Since then, at an uncertain hour,
> That agony returns:
> And till my ghastly tale is told,
> This heart within me burns.

More important than this sign of imperfect recovery is the contrast between the submissive sociability with which he must now content himself and the buoyancy of the voyager as he first set out. Such a voyage (of the sort that fascinated Coleridge in Anson's narratives) entails a self-reliant thrusting forth into the outer world and repudiates dependence on the comfort of ordinary social ties. But the intensity of Coleridge's need for the ties of affection seems to have set up anxiety about even the degree of independent assertiveness needed for any original achievement. Where we lament his life of wasted talent, he—in one mood—feared the acclaim that even his restricted use of his powers had brought him, and he ends his own epitaph

> Mercy for praise—to be forgiven for fame
> He asked, and hoped, through Christ. Do thou the same!

The bold independence of the voyager was for Coleridge only one step from an outrageous self-sufficiency which will wantonly destroy the ties of affection. The albatross is killed, and then the penalty must be paid in remorse, dejection, and the sense of being a worthless social outcast.

My account of 'The Ancient Mariner' would seem psychologically naïve and superficial to those who attach themselves more closely to one or other of the systems of depth psychology. In a Freudian study ('A dream, a vision, and a poem', *Yearbook of Psychoanalysis* VIII, ed. S. Lorand, New York, 1952) David Beres states his aim as being 'to understand the poet's fantasy in relation to his life history, to seek out the unconscious motivations of his creative art. To achieve this I propose to search in the poem, in the artist's other creations and in his life for evidence of unconscious psychic activity.' In speaking of understanding 'the poet's fantasy in relation to his life history' he leaves it doubtful whether he wants to understand the fantasy—a literary aim—or to understand the relation between the fantasy and the poet's life history, which would be largely a clinical and biographical undertaking. In the essay itself he shows that he does intend to enhance our understanding of the poem.

His interpretation, which is rather confusedly presented, rests on the view that Coleridge found his mother an intensely ambivalent object, and that though he said on one occasion that he had been his mother's darling he felt in the main unloved by her and experienced an unsatisfied 'need that manifested itself in a search for warmth, love and food'. There is some evidence of his over-preoccupation with food in childhood; and in later life he became, in Beres' words, '. . . a man who remained in his relationship to persons a never-satisfied, ever-demanding infant', one manifestation of this characteristic being his habit of borrowing. At the conscious level the ambivalence of mother-figures was handled by the common process of splitting the good and bad aspects, with idealized women (such as Mrs Evans, an idealized mother-image) worshipped from afar, and Mrs Fricker, his mother-in-law, as the bad, hated mother. Examining *Christabel* along Freudian lines, Beres finds evidence there too of conflict about the mother, including unconscious murderous wishes, sexual fantasies and the idea of a dangerous, formidably masculine mother, the 'phallic mother' in Freudian terminology.

Whether or not we accept such interpretations and employ the Freudian concepts and phraseology, it is still easy enough to suppose that Coleridge was—as many people have been—in a state of rather severe conflict about his mother and the reflections of her that he found in other women. Beres is probably right in his summarizing statement that '. . . Coleridge did not permit his hostile feelings to his mother to come to the surface of his conscious mind. He repressed in his unconscious mind his conflicted ambivalent emotions about her, his crying need, his bitter frustration, and his guilt at the hate this must have engendered.'

Turning to 'The Ancient Mariner', Beres now concentrates on the Albatross, emphasising that 'It ate the food it ne'er had eat', and associating this with a letter in which Coleridge spoke of his reluctance to trap mice with toasted cheese, exclaiming 'oh foul breach of the laws of hospitality', just as the gloss to the poem says that the Mariner 'inhospitably' kills the bird. This I can accept as interesting and fairly significant. From this, however, Beres moves—perhaps skids would be the better word—to an identification of the Albatross with the mother, saying 'Are not both creatures who bring protection and plenty?' He offers no further evidence from the poem. He simply repeats that the Albatross is 'an object associated with food and protection', undeterred by the fact that it was a receiver, not a giver of food. The lines in which the Albatross is referred to as 'him' ('He loved the bird that loved the man Who shot him with his bow') fail to give him pause. They only confirm his view that the mother with whom Coleridge was unconsciously preoccupied was a phallic mother. He writes:

> Coleridge strengthens the concept of the phallic mother by his use of the symbolism of the snake. By its behavior and by its relation to food and protection the Albatross is the mother, but in one line in the poem is identified as 'him'. To Coleridge, the father was a feminine giving male; the mother a masculine,

66

rejecting female. The Mariner at first despised the snakes; the child attempted to fight off the dangerous phallus, to deny his passive impulses; but it was a hopeless struggle. The Mariner must submit. What was ugly becomes beautiful. . . . And with submission the spell begins to break. . . .

This strikes me as a clear instance of psychological doctrines being imported into the interpretation, the facts of the poem being racked to make them fit. Coleridge's Albatross—as distinct from Beres'—is given a role much more like that of a child than a mother: it received food,

> And every day, for food or play,
> Came to the mariner's hollo!

But in fact its great significance lies in its being the only company in all that terrifying wilderness, which Coleridge describes in his gloss as 'The land of ice, and of fearful sounds, where no living thing was to be seen.' Its great significance was that it mitigated the isolation:

> At length did cross an Albatross:
> Thorough the fog it came;
> As if it had been a Christian soul,
> We hailed it in God's name.

In that very general sense it does possess an essential characteristic of the mother, in being a safeguard against the threat of loneliness, but it shares this characteristic with innumerable other forms of life, including children and pets who are really at the mercy of one's aggressive impulses in a way that the mother in reality is not. No doubt the value the Albatross represents is a value first experienced in the mother-child relation, but we are helped more by associating it with the mouse that the prisoner in solitary confinement comes to value for its company and the mice that Coleridge felt remorse about trapping. In objecting to an account such as Beres offers, we have to distinguish between the general psychoanalytic guesswork, which may be plausible as a clinical account of Coleridge, and the crude and inaccurate handling of the poem itself.

It seems likely enough that Coleridge's extreme susceptibility to feelings of guilt about any apparent disdain of friendliness and affection was ultimately the outcome of his relations with his mother in very early life, when he presumably experienced in specially acute form the usual problems of establishing psychological self-reliance and independence without losing the affection that originally goes with dependence. It follows that in a poem concerned with guilt arising from wanton aggression against a creature who offered love, mother-figures or -symbols are likely to be prominent. But although Beres is right in drawing attention to the mother-figures, his account is an over-simplification. He writes, '. . . the image of the mother appears as the Avenger, the Spectre-Woman, Life-in-Death, and as the forgiving "Holy Mother" who brings rain and sleep. The mother whom he restores to life brings him back to the safety of his homeland. A mother-figure forgives the crime against the mother.' This summary seems inaccurate. In the first place the Avenger is the Polar Spirit; 'Life-in-Death' is only the condition of guilt-ridden existence (dictated by Fate in the throw of the dice) which constitutes the punishment (though admittedly it may have been significant in Coleridge's psychopathology that this condition should be symbolized by the Mariner's becoming the property of a woman). In the second place to speak of 'the forgiving "Holy Mother" ' misses the point that the Mariner never has been forgiven. We are told in the gloss 'that penance long and heavy for the ancient mariner hath been accorded to the Polar Spirit'. The curse of his shipmates, the public condemnation, 'is finally expiated', but the far more terrible private conviction of guilt is never removed.

Although he is shriven by the Hermit, the penance of repeatedly reliving the voyage and re-experiencing his guilt and horror is the perpetual penance of a man who can never forgive himself. Coleridge is engaged in a subtler experience of guilt and remorse than Beres conveys in saying 'The mother whom he restores to life brings him back to the safety of his homeland.' The poem itself is clinically more exact and penetrating than the elaboration that Beres offers.

Maud Bodkin (in *Archetypal Patterns in Poetry*, London, 1934) applies to 'The Ancient Mariner' the ideas of Jung's psychology, especially the view that there are universal symbols and symbolic situations that recur in literature because they are part of the collective unconscious. We may reject the idea of the collective unconscious but still agree that, for other reasons, there are recurrent symbols in folk-lore, art and literature that often have much the same significance, in spite of being found geographically and historically far apart.

The literary question is how far it is profitable to come to a work of art with ideas drawn from other sources as to the significance of the symbols we are going to meet with. To some extent we must do this, some symbols being well-established parts of our cultural background. Voyaging into strange seas, for instance, the starting point of Coleridge's poem, has conventional implications and echoes that no one is likely to miss and that the poet would count upon in his readers. We can go a little farther, and usefully perhaps, with Maud Bodkin in noticing that wind and calm are, as she says, 'symbols of the contrasted states he [Coleridge] knew so poignantly, of ecstasy and of dull inertia'. It seems doubtful, though, whether we are much helped at this point by reminders of the uses to which the symbol of wind has been put in other literature; it may perhaps enrich our emotional associations to

Coleridge's wind and calm, but on the whole the emotional value of those natural events seems to be sufficiently conveyed by the context of the poem alone without going far beyond it to wider literary contexts.

Sharper doubts arise about the use Maud Bodkin makes of her chief idea, that the poem revolves round the widespread and ancient theme of rebirth. We should all agree that rebirth, in some broad sense that includes the kind of recovery the Mariner makes, is an important part of the poem. But Maud Bodkin embarks on a rather rambling and generalized account of ideas and images of rebirth as they occur in everyday experience and in literature, and she draws on other pieces of literature to build up her own emotive, quasi-creative account of the rebirth theme. All this is centred on Coleridge's poem but its relation to it is left nebulous. To quote her summary of what she has said is not quite fair, since some of her detailed comments are useful and sharply focused on the poem, but the summary does reveal the swamp of generalities in which one may flounder through following this method. She says that the poem communicates 'relations not easily detached for separate consideration from the total experience of the poem, but which we may recall in some such form as this: that the beauty of life is revealed amid the slime, that the glory of life is renewed after stagnation, that through the power of speech the values achieved by life are made immortal'. The objection to this is not only that it might equally well be summarizing a poem by Patience Strong, but also that the importation into the poem of the generalized Jungian idea of rebirth has seriously distorted her understanding of what Coleridge presents. For although the Mariner recovers from the depths of depression and the conviction that his own and every form of life is worthless, still he returns only to a guilt-haunted half-life, always in the power of the Nightmare Life-in-Death. To label this 'rebirth' and mobilize around it all the other uses of the theme in literature is not to throw light on the poem but to surround it with a foggy luminosity that conceals its outlines and texture.

We can hardly read 'The Ancient Mariner' now without being influenced by what is in some sense a psychological approach. If we accept the views of depth psychology we have to consider the likelihood that much of the poem has a symbolic significance that the writer was not fully aware of and certainly did not circumscribe and focus sharply as the writer of an allegory or parable does. (The following essay discusses this more fully.) But still he must be given the credit and the responsibility for what is there in the poem and what it does to the reader. He was content, for reasons that may not have been fully conscious to him, to leave the poem as it stands, and this is the poem he wanted us to read. We are face to face with what he actually said, not with what he could have consciously described as his intentions.

The dangers of the psychological approach, of which I have given examples (some, no doubt, unwittingly), arise from a failure to give close enough attention to what precisely the poem says. Precision here includes a response to subtlety and emotional shading, and it precludes the drawing out of remote meanings from one fragment of the poem without regard to the control exercised over it by the rest. In brief any psychologizing we undertake must be controlled by the discipline of close and sensitive reading; it can never compensate for a lapse in literary vigilance.

4

Concrete Embodiment: Emblem and Symbol

THERE are several words in English, a surprisingly large number, for a story or picture that has a further meaning than the object or event it depicts. Among the commonest are allegory, parable, fable, emblem, symbol; a proverb too conveys a general meaning beyond its literal content, and similes and metaphors come into the same class of statements (or compressed statements) that are made not for their immediate meaning but for a further implied meaning. Tracking through the dictionary you find, closely related in sense, apologue, analogy, trope, figure, similitude, type, token. Not content with all these, we have in recent times added Freud's distinction between manifest content and latent meaning in dreams, and Jung's notion of the primordial image and archetype. Even more recently some communication theorists have added a few of their own.

Such a wealth of synonyms and partial synonyms suggests that the process of conveying a meaning beyond what is directly stated is one of the highly important features of ordinary language. It seems to be avoided only at two extremes: either in giving instructions or commands within circumscribed, particular situations; or in attempting the highly abstract statements of philosophy, law, science, mathematics and so on. But in ordinary conversation and narrative, and in fiction and poetry, it is in one form or another the natural mode of expression. For one thing, any event you choose to describe (whether in gossip or in fiction or drama) is interesting and is

72

evaluated in a particular way because it forms part of broader interests and structures of value; it exemplifies something general besides being a unique event and interesting in its own right. Much of the effectiveness of literature lies in its combining (sometimes with tension between them) these two aspects of its materials, their uniqueness and their representativeness. At one extreme we have the parable or allegory, where the uniqueness of the event is drastically subordinated to the general values it exemplifies; and at the other extreme the effort of some authors towards objectivity, the accurate reporting of realistic detail and the apparent subordination of the event's broader significance to its uniqueness as an event. Neither extreme can ever be reached; the curve is asymptotic. The effort after objectivity is always and inevitably affected by the author's unspoken interests, preconceptions and values; he must select, he must give emphasis, and the very fact of serial narrative means sequence and salience. Perhaps the other extreme is approached more closely: some allegory and personification have been so denatured that they amount to little more than an alternative form of abstract statement. But usually even the allegory or parable has some of its interest for us in the concrete detail of a unique situation: the prodigal son would fain have filled his belly with the husks that the swine did eat, and as he drew towards home, when he was yet a great way off, his father saw him, and had compassion, and ran to welcome him.

In the greater part of fiction and drama the interest of the events and people in their own right comes first; we grow uneasy if we feel that they have been sought out for the purpose of conveying or illustrating a theme. On the other hand we accept, as part of the technique of communication, the use of incidents that hint at a further meaning beyond themselves. The intended visit of

Tchehov's three sisters to Moscow or of Virginia Woolf's people to the lighthouse has this obvious kind of reference beyond the simple part it plays in the action. L. P. Hartley's *The Shrimp and the Anemone* takes its title from the incident in which the sensitive boy's tender distress for the half-engulfed shrimp leads his tougher, managing sister to attempt a rescue operation that only kills the anemone without saving the shrimp. This kind of symbolism in novels, often indicated in the title, has been standard practice at least since Henry James wrote *The Golden Bowl*. It is one way of giving concrete embodiment to a focal point of the author's interest.

We could refer to all this kind of thing as symbolism. But it makes for clearer discussion if we discriminate at least between two varieties of the process, for which I have rather arbitrarily chosen the terms 'emblem' and 'symbol'. The contrast I have in mind is, roughly speaking, between a representation that stands for something clearly definable and one that stands for something of which the general nature is evident but the precise range and boundaries of meaning are not readily specified, perhaps not usefully specified.

A convenient example of the contrast is provided by Cowper's poem 'The Castaway' and Coleridge's 'The Ancient Mariner', both of them late eighteenth-century poems, both of them making use of materials and incidents suggested by the narratives of sea voyages, and both expressing indirectly their authors' own experience of great distress. Cowper's distress was the worse of the two. He was psychotic, and though his depression and sense of worthlessness had intermissions he knew the threat of complete and final submergence in despair. Coleridge was extremely neurotic, had bouts of severe depression and led a life that was crippled with self-frustration, but he was always potentially recoverable and able to regain touch with normal standards of judgment. It was the experience of these forms of depression that was embodied in the poems. But the kind of embodiment was very different in the two.

'The Castaway' presents Cowper's plight in the simple, direct form of a parable, with the secondary meaning explicitly stated;

> Obscurest night involved the sky,
> The Atlantic billows roar'd,
> When such a destined wretch as I,
> Wash'd headlong from on board,
> Of friends, of hope, of all bereft,
> His floating home for ever left.

He goes on to describe the man's courageous but hopeless struggle to keep afloat, the good will of his companions who were nevertheless forced to scud on in the storm and could give him no effectual aid, and the inevitable end. In the last stanza he states again, and more fully, the emblematic meaning for himself, bringing out more clearly his own sense of having no hope from a divine mercy:

> No voice divine the storm allay'd,
> No light propitious shone,
> When, snatch'd from all effectual aid,
> We perish'd, each alone:
> But I beneath a rougher sea,
> And whelm'd in deeper gulfs than he.

They are deeper gulfs because the sailor lost only his bodily existence whereas Cowper in his psychotic phases was convinced of eternal damnation. The struggle against being overwhelmed was something Cowper knew, and the powerlessness of his friends to help him effectually, for all their good will. The parallel is still closer from the fact that the sailor had done nothing to deserve his fate; he is the victim of what seems an accident, just as it seems by human reckoning an accident that some are elect of God and some condemned, as Cowper believed that he was.

The effect of Cowper's parable or emblem is to convey more vividly what he might have expressed quite directly: his sense of a calamity that overwhelms him and isolates him from others in his doom. It conveys the experience more vividly for two reasons: first, the long-drawn-out months and years of waiting for the return of the depressive delusions and the anticipated damnation are compressed into the brief accident and the doomed man's single hour of struggling; second, the obscure and hardly describable distress of mental and spiritual submergence is represented by the simple physical calamity of drowning. Some of the materials of the poem, it is true, may well have more obscure symbolic significance, the sea itself, for example. And there may be some doubt whether the calamity Cowper was referring to was his eternal damnation or his inevitable relapse into madness; we might perhaps say that he was unwittingly telling himself the truth, that his madness and only his madness *was* his damnation. And yet whatever complexities may lurk in the poem the main effect is of the fairly straightforward parable, with the drowning sailor as a central emblem.

'The Ancient Mariner' is very different from Cowper's poem in its way of embodying the author's experience. It is for one thing much more obscure and inexplicit. I have given (in the previous essay) what seems the essential theme, but there remain a large number of details of which the symbolic significance, if they have any, is much more difficult to guess at, and there are still more details and incidents which probably have no significance beyond themselves and beyond giving concreteness to the scene and heightening the air of the supernatural.[1] While it is true that a ballad about a haunted voyage would have had little continuing power if it had not embodied the experiences of depression and guilt which are among our human hazards, still it is equally true that a direct account of those experiences would have made nothing like so effective a poem; as Coleridge actually demonstrated in 'The Pains of Sleep' which, for all its interest as a direct personal statement, fails to have anything like the force of 'The Ancient Mariner'.

That force depends partly on the fact that in 'The Ancient Mariner' we have at least three sorts of things: there is direct narrative and an evocation of the appeal that things have in themselves (especially a delight in wonderful and beautiful natural appearances); then there are fairly explicit emblems, such as the dead Albatross hung round the Mariner's neck; but thirdly there is an intermediate range of objects and incidents which, besides being interesting in themselves are enriched by our impression that they have some further significance, though the nature of it may be difficult to indicate and its limits almost impossible to define. It is this third kind of object or incident that I call symbolic rather than emblematic. As examples from 'The Ancient Mariner' we might take the moon, with its curious changes of character during the poem; and we might ask why the background of the narrative is a wedding feast—why not a church service or a burial or a cattle fair or the embarkation of a vessel? What Coleridge has in fact chosen to use seems absolutely acceptable and appropriate; but if we try to say why we may have to explore its symbolic value. I will come back later to the moon and the wedding feast and see what can be said about them.

[1] Since this essay was written a useful selection of criticism and interpretation has appeared in *The Rime of the Ancient Mariner: A Handbook,* edited by Royal G. Gettmann, San Francisco, 1961.

I had supposed that at this point I should be able to quote usefully from Susanne Langer's *Philosophy in a New Key* (London, 1951). I am not sure now that she does deal precisely with what I have in mind. The general drift of her argument, though, is very relevant, and especially her denial of the common assumption 'That everything that is not speakable thought, is feeling'. She insists that 'there are things which do not fit the grammatical scheme of expression. But they are not necessarily blind, inconceivable, mystical affairs; they are simply matters which require to be conceived through some symbolic schema other than discursive language.' And after considering how extensively a language depends on metaphor and faded metaphor (even for utilitarian purposes) she remarks that with the progress of conceptual thinking and social communication 'Speech becomes increasingly discursive, practical, prosaic, until human beings can actually believe that it was invented as a utility, and was later embellished with metaphors for the sake of a cultural product called poetry.'

We can certainly agree that strictly defined, delimited language is a highly sophisticated and artificially constructed tool for the special purposes of science, philosophy or everyday utility. For all those purposes we have to pare away innumerable possible meanings from the words we use. That becomes very clear if one associates freely with the word for any common object. Take the word 'apple' for instance: the fruit of course, but then Eve's apple, apples of desire, stay me with flagons, comfort me with apples, Atalanta's golden apples, the apple a day that keeps the doctor away, rosy-cheeked apples, cankered apples, Dead Sea apples, the apple of his eye—and so endlessly on. All the varieties of the object, all the implications it has gained in particular contexts, public and private, all that the object suggests by resemblance, all that the word suggests by sound-association have to be stripped away for the special purposes of the botanist and the fruiterer. It is their strict delimitation of meaning which is the specialized, 'unnatural' use; an enormous number of processes set off in us by the word have to be inhibited for purposes of utility or exact thinking. In literature and everyday conversation the context controls the range of implied meaning but it is always a question how rigorously the reader or listener should inhibit the less immediately relevant meanings and associations of the words. It may be hard to decide where the author or speaker intends the line to be drawn between the relevant and the irrelevant.

What is true of words is true of incidents too. It is difficult to be sure at what point their symbolic meaning is to be considered as exhausted. The author himself may be far from certain. T. S. Eliot has spoken of the two-way traffic between the dramatist and his characters: though in a sense he creates his character he also finds that it draws out of him potentialities of which he may have known nothing before. In the same way what the poet actually writes may far outrun anything that he was capable of intending before he wrote. If the event he uses is only an emblem both he and the reader will know pretty clearly what it means and what it does not mean. They can translate it. The meaning is detachable from the object or event that represents it. If it is in my sense a symbol we may neither of us, reader or author, be confident in detaching a limited, translatable meaning, because we are not certain what aspects of the event and what associations of the words describing it can be ruled out as irrelevant.

This characteristic of symbolism is evident in some of the best of Wordsworth. Although it gets quoted to the point of tedium I must use as an illustration the famous passage about the mountain that seemed to rise up and follow Wordsworth when as a boy he took someone's boat on the lake without permission. I take his passage partly because there has been some misunderstanding, even by people who admire it, of what Wordsworth was doing here.

After evoking the boy's pleasure in rowing, he goes on

... lustily

> I dipped my oars into the silent lake,
> And, as I rose upon the stroke, my boat
> Went heaving through the water like a swan;
> When, from behind that craggy steep till then
> The horizon's bound, a huge peak, black and huge,
> As if with voluntary power instinct,
> Upreared its head. I struck and struck again,
> And growing still in stature the grim shape
> Towered up between me and the stars, and still,
> For so it seemed, with purpose of its own
> And measured motion like a living thing,
> Strode after me. With trembling oars I turned
> Back to the covert of the willow tree;
> There in her mooring-place I left my bark,—
> And through the meadows homeward went, in grave
> And serious mood ...

Wordsworth makes it quite clear that the huge peak stands for an admonitory and perhaps retributive moral authority. E. M. W. Tillyard (in *Poetry, Direct and Oblique*, London, 1934) goes this far in his reading of the passage, but he assumes that this is all, and that Wordsworth has been creating what I should call an emblem. Tillyard writes:

> In this description he has practically created the grandest possible moral symbol out of a piece of nature. Yet he never again makes use of it. The crag with its wealth of possible significance is allowed to drop out of his poetical property and relapses into the mere description of a scene. This is but one example of what is really a heart-breaking waste of potential meaning.

If Wordsworth had done as Tillyard suggests and used the peak with the same meaning in other contexts he would have invited a simple process of decoding: when we met a reference to a huge black peak we should have known that it stood for 'guardian of morals or externalized conscience', just as when we hear a certain pattern of dots and dashes we know that it stands for S O S and that someone needs help. Tillyard in fact seems to assume that we have here a meaning that can be detached from its context. But the avoidance of what he asks for has been a central feature of much of the most interesting writing in English. When he says that the crag 'relapses into the mere description of a scene' he fails to recognize that by being embedded in a particular scene and event the peak has a much more subtle and complex—and a more un-certain—meaning than it could have had as a moral emblem drawn from nature.

This 'grandest possible moral symbol' is in its concrete presentation a very questionable thing. Writing retro-spectively in the lines that introduce the whole passage, Wordsworth does, it is true, take the experience to have been one of the 'severer interventions' by which Nature formed his character, but the experience itself, as he re-constructs it, is much more ambiguous. The taking of the boat was a rather small offence. Its wrongness is men-tioned very briefly—'It was an act of stealth And troubled pleasure'—and the exhilaration of rowing is conveyed with much more intensity. The result is that the really tremendous threat suggested by the huge upreared moun-tain seems out of proportion. Nor is it at first an effective hint to his conscience; he tries to escape by rowing harder, and only when the grim shape seems actually to pursue him does he give in and turn back with trembling oars.

In whatever way the reflective Wordsworth may wish to interpret the incident it seems in reality to have been

far different from a benignly severe admonition of a small
fault. From our vantage point it looks much more like the
irrational and savage threatening of what Freud called the
super-ego, not the pricking of a reasonable conscience.
That modern interpretation is not necessary. All that
matters is that in reading the passage we should notice
that whatever is symbolized is far from simple and that
the central object, the menacing peak, is totally different
from a moral emblem that can be detached and used else-
where with the same meaning; for in the context of the
whole passage we can scarcely be sure what the boundaries
of its meaning are.

Several other passages of Wordsworth's poetry provide
instances of this uninterpreted symbolism—this transi-
tional form between on the one hand explicit allegory and
on the other the reporting of entirely concrete experience
for its own interest without secondary implications. The
first of the Lucy poems is a striking example. When the
moon seems to drop suddenly behind Lucy's cottage, the
lover is made to underline the possibility that the event
suggested:

> 'O mercy!', to myself I cried,
> 'If Lucy should be dead!'

The sudden extinction of the light on which his eyes had
been fixed while 'In one of those sweet dreams I slept' is
the appropriate symbolic introduction to the sequence
that ends with a superbly bare confrontation of the fact of
grief and loss in 'A slumber did my spirit seal'. The
symbolic reference of the first experience—the steadily
descending moon, the almost tranced man watching it
and journeying on as if guided by it, but not foreseeing
the end of its descent—is certainly not exhausted by the
meaning that the lover's cry makes explicit. Nor does the
implication of the 'sweet dream' come out until we have

read 'A slumber did my spirit seal'. And yet the compelling quality of the poem depends not just on the symbolic meanings, which might be commonplace in paraphrase, but on the vividness and particularity of the experience in which they have been implied.

The same fact appears in a poem called 'Nutting' written at about the same time as the Lucy poems. It describes the fierce joy with which as a boy, after finding an untouched nook full of richly laden hazels, the poet tore down and ravaged the trees; and it speaks of the regret that he thinks he felt when he saw the nook and the green and mossy bower 'deformed and sullied'. He presents the incident as a fragment of autobiography, simply reporting the actual experience, but it obviously has symbolic application over a wide range. Its possible sexual references are brought out clearly, and I imagine intentionally, but beyond that it suggests much more generally an aggressive and avid approach to the world, the ruthless satisfaction of desire without thought of the consequences to the helpless, and the way in which the sense of ruthless ravage even adds to the pleasure of satisfying the desire; at the same time it shows this spirit accompanying, perhaps actually enhanced by, a capacity for recognizing the beauty of what is eventually spoilt:

> Then up I rose,
> And dragged to earth both branch and bough, with crash
> And merciless ravage: and the shady nook
> Of hazels, and the green and mossy bower,
> Deformed and sullied, patiently gave up
> Their quiet being: and unless I now
> Confound my present feeling with the past,
> Ere from the mutilated bower I turned
> Exulting, rich beyond the wealth of kings,
> I felt a sense of pain when I beheld
> The silent trees, and saw the intruding sky.

The possible implications of simple incidents are extensive, and it must always be difficult to say just how far they should be unfolded and claimed as part of a poem's meaning. Readers will differ in the amount of meaning they see in an event. They will differ also, perhaps even more, in their degree of conscious awareness of what is conveyed to them; they may grasp in some non-verbal form much more than they could paraphrase. Here we reach a question that constantly arises in the reading of modern poetry where obscurity is tolerated and almost expected: is it useful to say that the extended meanings are part of the poem, and have we any safeguard against attributing to it almost endlessly extended meanings that may be no more than one reader's private projections?

The answer is presumably twofold. In the first place, none of the wider implications are of literaray importance unless they enrich our reading of the poem itself; however much we draw out extended meanings we have to be sure that they can be telescoped back into the poem and be present to us when we read it again—present to us with immediacy, not through a secondary process of reflection or decoding. Some of the exegesis of Blake's poetry fails to survive the test of this requirement that the extended meaning must be fused with the poem, not an outgrowth from it (cf. p. 34 above). This in turn suggests the second part of the answer. Whatever implied symbolic meanings we claim to see must be shown as arising from particular features of the poem and tethered firmly to the poet's own words. Scrupulous attention to the poem will commonly remind us how much of it is concerned with experience in one unique situation and how subordinate, in one sense, the extended meanings are. The poem can be compared to an object of definite unique shape, lit from behind by a point of light and casting a shadow that grows larger and vaguer as it gets further from the object, and a shadow too that will alter to some extent according to the contours of the minds and the cultural epochs it falls on. When we claim that an extended shadow-meaning comes from a poem we must be prepared to trace it back to the exact outline of the poet's words, to the precise object that the poem is. When we do that with a poem like 'Nutting' we find at once that what Wordsworth wrote about was the experience of one young boy when he was nutting on one particular occasion. Much of the force and vigour of the poem depends on that, and many of its details belong only to that level of meaning, even though it may have been remoter implied meanings that made the incident worth re-creating.

When inexplicit symbolism is used extensively in poetry we face the danger not only of idiosyncratic interpretation on the reader's part but of bogus profundity on the author's. There are too many ways of producing something that looks mysteriously symbolic, and when valid obscurity has a recognized place in any of the arts techniques of mystification, too, are bound to thrive. It is not enough simply to express our conviction that what we read is significant and invite others to read and agree with us; Eliot seems too easily content with that method in introducing St-J. Perse's *Anabasis* (London, 1930). Although he may well be right in some sense when he says 'There is a logic of the imagination as well as a logic of concepts', it is scarcely enough merely to advise the reader 'to allow the images to fall into his memory successively without questioning the reasonableness of each at the moment; so that, at the end, a total effect is produced.' I think we must manage to articulate more than that if we are to reach any secure consensus, or to discriminate between serious work and the bogus (especially the unintentionally bogus), or to decide whether a reader is getting from a poem anything like as much as he could get. We may be able only to fumble in the direction of what we think is there, but we have to try, and we can reasonably expect from the author some materials on which to base our attempt. At the very least we ought to be able to say what it is in his writing that gives the impression that a symbolic meaning is being offered, and from that it should be possible to make a start towards saying what sort of meaning is suggested.

With this in mind I want to look more closely at Coleridge's use of the moon in 'The Ancient Mariner'. That it has some significance beyond being a mere feature of the mise-en-scène is clear from the part it plays at the turning point of the poem when the Mariner emerges from his despairing disgust with all forms of life. The marginal glosses emphasize the point. Beside the lines

> And a thousand thousand slimy things
> Lived on; and so did I

the gloss reads 'He despiseth the creatures of the calm'. Eight stanzas later, when he begins to notice their beauty, the gloss runs 'By the light of the moon he beholdeth God's creatures of the great calm'. They are the same creatures, first despised, then seen as God's creatures. It is first in the moonlight that he notices the flashing of the water-snakes, and the only change that has occurred between the two stanzas lies in his attention to the moon. The change is made the pivot of the poem, with a sudden transition in sense and rhythm from a crescendo of horror to the exquisitely peaceful, lulling description of the rising moon, only a rime word tying the two stanzas together:

> An orphan's curse would drag to hell
> A spirit from on high;
> But oh! more horrible than that
> Is a curse in a dead man's eye!

86

> Seven days, seven nights, I saw that curse,
> And yet I could not die.

> The moving Moon went up the sky,
> And nowhere did abide:
> Softly she was going up,
> And a star or two beside—

The emotional change, which the verse suggests, the gloss makes explicit. Instead of bitterness and disgust and self-reproach, the Mariner experiences a yearning towards the moon and the stars that accompany her, secure of welcome wherever they are. It seems obviously a maternal quality that he recognizes in the moon; and that symbolism is confirmed when a few stanzas later—with the poem's characteristic fusion of pagan and Christian thought—the Mariner exclaims

> To Mary Queen the praise be given!
> She sent the gentle sleep from Heaven,

and the gloss says that the rain too came 'By grace of the holy Mother'. The holy Mother is thanked for what the moon has initiated.

In this section of the poem, then, we could say that the moon is a rather straightforward emblem of maternal assurance. But in other parts the context gives it a different quality, and we have to notice greater complexity in what it suggests. The developing ill-fate of the Mariner and his ship is accompanied by

> The horned Moon, with one bright star
> Within the nether tip,

and in the light of the star-dogged moon his ship-mates die. Coleridge noted on one copy of the poem that 'It is a common superstition among sailors "that something evil is about to happen, whenever a star dogs the Moon" '

(*The Road to Xanadu*, p. 182 note). Consequently we must say that if the moon is a maternal symbol here too, it now hints at a less benign aspect of the mother, or at an attitude towards her that makes her into an evil influence. Between the one passage and the other, the relation of the stars to the moon has decidedly changed. In the first, the close accompaniment of the star is seen as an evil. In the second, the moon is still accompanied—'a star or two beside'—but now the suggestion is of willing companionship among independent people. If the moon is a mother symbol or emblem the accompanying stars are now like sons who enjoy independence without isolation; they are the lords who possess the sky, simultaneously journeying and at home. The hinted symbolism points towards the emotional gamut through which the relation between mother and child may move, the theme which David Beres in his Freudian analysis found in the poem.

After the turning point when the Mariner has come to see the moon as benign, the homeward journey proceeds with the moon keeping constant watch and guiding the sea:

> Still as a slave before his lord,
> The ocean hath no blast;
> His great bright eye most silently
> Up to the Moon is cast—
>
> If he may know which way to go;
> For she guides him, smooth or grim.
> See brother, see! how graciously
> She looketh down on him.

and when the ship reaches the home harbour the whole silent scene is illuminated by the moon.

The symbolic meanings are hinted, not clearly developed, nor delimited. All we are given is the broad area of human experience from which they are coming: the relation of the child to the mother and the tension between the wish for security and the wish for independent voyaging about the world. And I think we can say that the background of the narrative, the wedding feast, is at least consistent with this theme. A wedding represents a decisive departure from the home of childhood. The Wedding Guest is a buoyant young man—one of three Gallants—going to participate in the sending off ceremony. We hear 'the merry din' of the feast in stanza 2, and then four stanzas later the same atmosphere is recalled as the Mariner (who, of course, was not then Ancient) is sent off on his voyage:

> The ship was cheered, the harbour cleared,
> Merrily did we drop
> Below the kirk, below the hill,
> Below the lighthouse top.

It was the young Gallant, going merrily to launch his next of kin on adult life, who was so stunned by the story that he 'Turned from the Bridegroom's door'.

I think it would be a mistake in the technique of reading the poem—and the same applies to a great deal of modern poetry—if we took the moon or anything else as an emblem and tried to interpret everything closely as an allegory. Equally it would be a mistake to overlook the likelihood that the force and fascinating quality of parts of the poem come from their hint of symbolic meaning, their hint of a direction in which to look for more than a literal meaning. Part of the technique of such poetry consists in its refusal to specify how far we are to go in the indicated direction. But our enjoyment is fuller when we identify the general direction from which associations and echoes, clear or faint, are coming.

The author need not have been aware, in any other terms than those of the poem itself, what hinted sense he was conveying. He was content to leave the poem as we have it; and if we can demonstrate that these associations and suggestions are there, still more if we can show them to be to some extent coherently organized, we can at least plausibly assume that their presence played some part in the total satisfaction the author found in his work.

5

Aspects of the Poetry of Isaac Rosenberg

I. TREATMENT OF WAR EXPERIENCE

WHAT most distinguishes Isaac Rosenberg from other English poets who wrote of the 1914-1918 war is the intense significance he saw in the kind of living effort that the war called out, and the way in which his technique enabled him to present both this and the suffering and the waste as inseparable aspects of life in war. Further, there is in his work, without the least touch of coldness, nevertheless a certain impersonality: he tried to feel in the war a significance for life as such, rather than seeing only its convulsion of the human life he knew.

Occasionally, it is as well to say at once, he seems to simplify his experience too much, letting the suffering be swallowed up, though at his best he knows it never can be, in glory; this happens in 'The Dead Heroes', and to some extent in 'Soldier' and 'Marching'. By themselves these poems might have implied a lack of sensitiveness; actually they were in him only one side of an effort after a more complete sensitivity. He could at least as easily have written only of loss and suffering:

> Here is one not long dead.
> His dark hearing caught our far wheels,
> And the choked soul stretched weak hands
> To reach the living word the far wheels said;
> The blood-dazed intelligence beating for light,
> Crying through the suspense of the far torturing wheels . . .

The significance which the war held for Rosenberg might have been anticipated from his dissatisfaction with the pre-war social order (especially acute, it seems, in South Africa where he was living when the war came). The poem he wrote on first hearing of the war makes evident at once his deep division of feeling: on the one hand,

> In all men's hearts it is:
> Some spirit old
> Hath turned with malign kiss
> Our lives to mould.

but also,

> O ancient crimson curse!
> Corrode, consume;
> Give back this universe
> Its pristine bloom.

His dissatisfaction with pre-war life had already shown itself in his work, notably in the revolt against God which appears in several passages, God being taken as someone responsible for the condition of the world and its established order:

> Ah, this miasma of a rotting God!

And of the rotting God and his priests he exclaims:

> Who has made of the forest a park?
> Who has changed the wolf to a dog?
> And put the horse in harness?
> And man's mind in a groove?

In 'Moses', from which this passage comes, he was engrossed with the theme of revolt against a corrupting routine; he presents Moses at the moment of breaking free from the comfort of the usual and politic by killing the overseer. Rosenberg never fully defined his attitude to violence as distinct from strength, though there is a hint in his letters that 'The Unicorn' might have approached this question. In 'Moses' he accepts violence

92

because it seems a necessary aspect of any effort to bring back the power and vigour of purpose which he felt the lack of in civilized life:

> I have a trouble in my mind for largeness.

It was because of this attitude to the pre-war world that Rosenberg, hating the war, was yet unable to set against it the possibilities of ordinary civilian life, and regret them in the way, for instance, that Wilfred Owen could regret them in 'Strange Meeting'. When Rosenberg wanted to refer to an achieved culture—rather than merely human possibilities—against which to measure the work of war he had to go back to remote and idealized Jewish history, producing 'The Burning of the Temple' and 'The Destruction of Jerusalem by the Babylonian Hordes'. More usually he opposed both to the war and to the triviality of contemporary civilization only a belief in the possibilities of life and a hope derived from its more primitive aspects:

> Here are the springs, primeval elements,
> The roots' hid secrecy, old source of race,
> Unreasoned reason of the savage instinct.

The root is the most important of the symbols which recur throughout his work, and birth, creation, and growth are his common themes.

These and related themes were to have been worked out in the unfinished play, 'The Unicorn'. But there they would have been influenced vitally by the war, and Rosenberg's account in letters of what he intends the play to be helps to reveal the significance of the war to him. The existing fragments point to his plan having changed more than once, but the letters show something of what he aimed at. The play was to have included a kind of Sabine rape by a decaying race who had no women and yearned for continuity:

> When aged flesh looks down on tender brood;
> For he knows between his thin ribs' walls
> The giant universe, the interminable
> Panorama—synods, myths and creeds,
> He knows his dust is fire and seed.

At the same time he wanted the play 'to symbolize the war and all the devastating forces let loose by an ambitious and unscrupulous will' (which might have been essentially the will of Moses seen in a slightly different light). Moreover, 'Saul and Lilith are ordinary folk into whose ordinary lives the Unicorn bursts. It is to be a play of terror— terror of hidden things and the fear of the supernatural.' It would, in fact, have been closely related to 'Daughters of War':

> We were satisfied of our lords the moon and the sun
> To take our wage of sleep and bread and warmth—
> These maidens came—these strong everliving Amazons,
> And in an easy might their wrists
> Of night's sway and noon's sway the sceptres brake,
> Clouding the wild, the soft lustres of our eyes.

The complexity of feeling here, which would probably have been still more evident in 'The Unicorn', is typical of the best of Rosenberg's war poetry. His finest passages are not concerned exclusively either with the strength called out by war or with the suffering: they spring more directly from the events and express a stage of consciousness appearing before either simple attitude has become differentiated. They express, that is, what it is tempting to call, inaccurately, a 'blending' of the two attitudes. It can be seen in this:

> None saw their spirits' shadow shake the grass,
> Or stood aside for the half used life to pass
> Out of those doomed nostrils and the doomed mouth,
> When the swift iron burning bee
> Drained the wild honey of their youth.

It is noteworthy here that Rosenberg is able and content to present contrasted aspects of the one happening without having to resort to the bitterness or irony which are the easier attitudes to such a contrast. One sign and expression of his peculiar greatness consists in his being able, in spite of his sensitiveness, to do without irony. The last two lines of the passage just quoted come from a keyed-up responsiveness to the vividness of violent death in war, but the passage possesses nothing of nationalist-militarist rapture; it is 'the half used life' that passes; and then

> Burnt black by strange decay
> Their sinister faces lie,
> The lid over each eye;
> The grass and coloured clay
> More motion have than they,
> Joined to the great sunk silences.

Rosenberg seems to have been specially impressed by the destruction of men at the moment of a simplified greatness which they could never have reached before, their destruction by the very forces that had made human strength and endurance more vividly impressive than ever. This conception of the war he tried to express through the fiction of some intention being fulfilled in the destruction:

> Earth has waited for them,
> All the time of their growth
> Fretting for their decay:
> Now she has them at last!
> In the strength of their strength
> Suspended—stopped and held.

From this it was a short inevitable step to the suggestion of some vague immortality for these lives:

> What fierce imaginings their dark souls lit?
> Earth! Have they gone into you?

Somewhere they must have gone,
And flung on your hard back
Is their souls' sack,
Emptied of God-ancestralled essences.

'Daughters of War' develops the same group of ideas. 'Earth' gives place to the more active symbol of the Blakesque Amazonian spirits who take as lovers those who have been released from Earth,

From the doomed earth, from the doomed glee
And hankering of hearts.

The Daughters, their voices (as Rosenberg says in a letter) 'spiritual and voluptuous at the same time', are a symbolic expression of what he felt ought to be a possible plane of living. They are an embodiment of the God-ancestralled essences, but he feels now that they can be reached only through the sacrifice of men's defective humanity, that they bring about 'the severance of all human relationship and the fading away of human love'. This was an idea that he had been feeling towards in 'Girl to Soldier on Leave'. It is only for warriors that the Daughters wait, for the simplification of living effort which Rosenberg saw in the war impressed him as a first step—a step back—towards the primitive sources of life, 'the root side of the tree of life'. Death in itself was not his concern, but only death at the moment when life was simplified and intensified; this he felt had a significance which he represents by immortality. For him it was no more than the immortality of the possibilities of life.

This immortality and the value he glimpses in the living effort of war in no way mitigate his suffering at the human pain and waste. The value of what was destroyed seemed to him to have been brought into sight only by the destruction, and he had to respond to both facts without allowing either to neutralize the other. It is this which is most impressive in Rosenberg—the complexity of experience which he was strong enough to permit himself and which his technique was fine enough to reveal. Naturally there were some aspects of the war which he was not able to compass in his response: maiming and lingering death he never treats of—he thinks only in terms of death which comes quickly enough to be regarded as a single living experience. Nevertheless the complexity he did achieve constituted a large part of his importance as a poet.

To say that Rosenberg tried to understand all that the war stood for means probably that he tried to expose the whole of himself to it. In one letter he describes as an intention what he obviously achieved: 'I will not leave a corner of my consciousness covered up, but saturate myself with the strange and extraordinary new conditions of this life. . . .' This willingness—and ability—to let himself be new-born into the new situation, not subduing his experience to his established personality, is a large part, if not the whole secret of the robustness which characterizes his best work. ('Robustness' is, as the fragment on Emerson indicates, his own word for something he felt to be an essential of great poetry.) It was due largely, no doubt, to his lack of conviction of the adequacy of civilian standards. In 'Troopship' and 'Louse Hunting' there is no civilian resentment at the conditions he writes of. Here as in all the war poems his suffering and discomfort are unusually *direct*; there is no secondary distress arising from the sense that these things *ought not* to be. He was given up to realizing fully what *was*. He has expressed his attitude in 'The Unicorn':

> *Lilith:* I think there is more sorrow in the world
> Than man can bear.
> *Nubian:* None can exceed their limit, lady:
> You either bear or break.

97

It was Rosenberg's exposure of his whole personality that gave his work its quality of impersonality. Even when he imagines his brother's death he brings it into a poem which is equally concerned with the general destruction and the circumstances of life in war, and which ends with a generalization of his personal suffering:

> What are the great sceptred dooms
> To us, caught
> In the wild wave?
> We break ourselves on them,
> My brother, our hearts and years.

The same quality is present, most finely, in 'Break of day in the trenches':

> The darkness crumbles away—
> It is the same old druid time as ever.
> Only a live thing leaps my hand—
> A queer sardonic rat—
> As I pull the parapet's poppy
> To stick behind my ear.
> Droll rat, they would shoot you if they knew
> Your cosmopolitan sympathies
> (And God knows what antipathies).
>
> .   .   .   .   .
>
> It seems you inwardly grin as you pass
> Strong eyes, fine limbs, haughty athletes
> Less chanced than you for life,
>
> .   .   .   .   .
>
> Poppies whose roots are in man's veins
> Drop, and are ever dropping;
> But mine in my ear is safe,
> Just a little white with the dust.

There is here a cool distribution of attention over the rat, the poppy and the men which gives them all their due, is considerate of all their values, and conveys in their precise definition something of the impersonal immensity of a war. For Rosenberg the war was not an incident of his life, to be seen from without, but, instead, one kind of life, as unquestionable as any life.

II. HANDLING OF LANGUAGE

Without attempting a systematic survey of Rosenberg's use of language, it is perhaps useful to discuss briefly one feature of his writing which must seem important even in a first aproach to his work, partly because it contributes largely to his obscurity. It is that in much of his most interesting work he was only in a very special sense 'selecting words to express ideas'.

Usually when we speak of finding words to express a thought we seem to mean that we have the thought rather close to formulation and use it to measure the adequacy of any possible phrasing that occurs to us, treating words as servants of the idea. 'Clothing a thought in language', whatever it means psychologically, seems a fair metaphorical description of much speaking and writing. Of Rosenberg's work it would be misleading. He—like many poets in some degree, one supposes—brought language to bear on the incipient thought at an earlier stage of its development. Instead of the emerging idea being racked slightly so as to fit a more familiar approximation of itself, and words found for *that*, Rosenberg let it manipulate words almost from the beginning, often without insisting on the controls of logic and intelligibility. An example of what happened occurs in a prose fragment on Emerson and a parallel phrase in a letter. In these he tries two ways of describing some quality that he feels in Emerson: at one time he calls it 'light dancing in light', at another, trying to be more explicit and limit further the possible meanings of the phrase, he writes 'a beaminess, impalpable and elusive only in a circle.' The elements of this idea are apparently 'lightness' and 'elusiveness' and also 'end-lessness, continuity within itself' of some kind, and these elements he feels also to be inseparable and necessary to each other.

He would of course have worked further on this before considering it finished. Much of the labour he gave to writing—and he is known to have worked extremely hard —was devoted, as his letters show, to making these complex ideas intelligible without sacrificing their complexity. 'Now, when my things fail to be clear, I am sure it is because of the luckless choice of a word or the failure to introduce a word that would flash my idea plain, as it is to my own mind' (*Works*, p. 319). It is the creation of ideas which he takes to be his task as a poet; speaking of the cause of the faults in his poems he insists (*Works*, p. 373) that it is not 'blindness or carelessness; it is the brain succumbing to the herculean attempt to enrich the world of ideas'. And he is reported to have worked constantly towards concentrating more and more *sense* into his poetry, disturbed at the thought of thinness or emptiness. But how remote this was from implying any respect for mere intellectual exercising in verse is evident not only from his poetry but also from his own description of what he aimed at: poetry 'where an interesting complexity of thought is kept in tone and right value to the dominating idea so that it is understandable and still ungraspable' (*Works*, p. 371).

It remains 'ungraspable'—incapable of formulation in slightly different terms—because Rosenberg allowed his words to emerge from the pressure of a very wide context of feeling and only a very general direction of thought. The result is that he seems to leave every idea partly embedded in the undifferentiated mass of related ideas from which it has emerged. One way in which this effect came about was his rapid skimming from one metaphor to another, each of which contributes something of its implications—one can't be sure how much—before the next appears. A clear example—though not his best as poetry—occurs in 'Moses':

> Fine! Fine!
> See, in my brain
> What madmen have rushed through
> And like a tornado
> Torn up the tight roots
> Of some dead universe:
> The old clay is broken
> For a power to soak in and knit
> It all into tougher tissues
> To hold life;
> Pricking my nerves till the brain might crack
> It boils to my finger-tips,
> Till my hands ache to grip
> The hammer—the lone hammer
> That breaks lives into a road
> Through which my genius drives.

The compression which Rosenberg's use of language gave him is therefore totally unlike the compression of acute conversation—such for example as some of Siegfried Sassoon's verse offers—in which a highly differentiated idea is presented through the most effective *illustration* that can be found. Rosenberg rarely or never illustrated his ideas by writing; he reached them through writing.

With this as his attitude to language it is not surprising that he should have had the habit of reworking phrases and images again and again, developing out of them meanings which were not 'the' meaning he had originally wanted to 'express' with them. Emerging, as they seem to have done, from a wide context of feeling, his more interesting images carried with them a richer or subtler meaning than Rosenberg could feel he had exhausted in one poem, and he would therefore use them again in another. This happened with 'Heights of night ringing with unseen larks', a phrase that first reports an actual incident during the war, and is then used by the Nubian in 'The Unicorn' to contrast the mystery-exploiting femininity of his own girls with the vividness of Lilith:

> Our girls have hair
> Like heights of night ringing with never-seen larks,
> Or blindness dim with dreams:
> Here is a yellow tiger gay that blinds your night.

Moreover in the first of these poems he had said that the dropping of the larks' song when death might as easily have dropped was

> Like a blind man's dreams on the sand
> By dangerous tides;
> Like a girl's dark hair, for she dreams no ruin lies there . . .

It is this reworking of images—developing first one set of possibilities and then another—which gives one the impression of Rosenberg's having as it were modelled in language.

The idea of a sack for the soul is similarly reworked and developed. It occurs twice in 'Moses': first simply, 'we give you . . . skin sacks for souls', as a contemptuous description of the Hebrew slaves; then the soul sack becomes the body and the habits of ordinary life to be thrown off in Moses' spiritual development:

> Soul-sack fall away
> And show what you hold!

And finally the emptiness and collapsedness of the sack allows it to be used of the bodies of the dead flung on the earth:

> And flung on your hard back
> Is their souls' sack,
> Emptied of God-ancestralled essences.

'God-ancestralled essences' in turn reappear in 'The Unicorn' where they are said to be contaminated by

> . . . a crazed shadow from no golden body
> That poisons at the core
> What smiles may stray.

The obscurity of this is relieved if one sees that it comes from an earlier poem beginning:

> Crazed shadows, from no golden body
> That I can see. . . .

and ending:

> And poison at the core
> What smiles may stray.

That poem deals with evil abroad at night—shadows forming without any 'golden body' as source of light—and in 'The Unicorn' the ideas have been remodelled so as to suggest the humdrum middle-aged evil of Saul which is mauling Lilith's love and beauty.

All this may only amount to saying that when Rosenberg got a good phrase he tried to make the most of it, though it equally suggests what an interesting process making the most of a phrase may be. Naturally, too, it need not be supposed that Rosenberg was unique or even —among poets—very unusual in treating language in this way. What is unusual, however, is his willingness to publish several uses of the same phrase or image (and there are many more instances than I have quoted), so that what may be a fairly common process is, in Rosenberg's work, available for examination. Moreover, although the process may be familiar in the writing of poetry, it is by no means usual in ordinary language, and there can be no doubt that it has special significance as a means of exploring and ordering the affective sources from which we draw our more manageable mental life.

6

Words and Meanings: a Note on Eliot's Poetry

... the intolerable wrestle
With words and meanings.
('East Coker')

THE obscurities of Eliot's poetry are of different kinds. One results from the suppression of connecting links between statements or evoked images, the suppression in which Ezra Pound encouraged him and which he approves of in St-J. Perse. The second comes from ambiguity; two meanings, neither in itself obscure, are offered by the same phrase. The third and most interesting is the direct and necessary outcome of attempting extremely difficult statements.

The first kind has often been discussed and a good deal of exegesis consists in guesses about the suppressed links. That indeed points to the inherent danger of the method: besides achieving vividness and concreteness it offers too inviting a challenge to crossword-intelligence, just as Eliot's use of allusion may make understanding abdicate to erudition. From his Preface to the translation of *Anabasis* it sounds as though Eliot maintains the possibility of judging the appropriateness of a sequence of images and ideas without knowing or guessing what implied statement is linking them. Perhaps inevitably, he gives no clue to the criterion by which we 'distinguish between order and chaos in the arrangement of images'; he only says that people who do not appreciate poetry find it difficult to make the distinction. He recommends repeated readings to reach conviction about the imaginative ordering. But presumably people who do not appreciate poetry might well accept as ordered an imaginative chaos that had come to slide acceptably through their minds as the result of mere familiarization.

The fact is that much still remains to be understood about the non-discursive forms of mental organization and how far they can be independent of an implied discursive scaffolding. In many of Eliot's earlier poems (such, say, as 'A Cooking Egg' and 'Sweeney Among the Nightingales') it is evident from the efforts of the commentators that there had been a scaffolding though it was removed in the course of construction. And the minor intellectual poets easily passed from this kind of thing to cryptogramic cleverness.

Obscurity arising from the omission of explanatory links justifies itself by giving greater compression and vividness. The uncertainty produced by ambiguity serves at its best a different purpose: it is a way round the intolerable fact that in saying one thing you exclude other things, allied but different, that had equal claim to be heard in the same context. At less than its best it may result in a conflict of senses between which a choice should have been made, as to my mind it does once in Eliot's work at a point to which Helen Gardner has drawn attention (more appreciative than mine). She points out that in the lines

> . . . the perpetual star
> Multifoliate rose
> Of death's twilight kingdom
> The hope only
> Of empty men.

the construction leaves 'only' ambiguous. It may mean either that the star, the Christian symbol, is a hope held by none but empty men; or that for empty men the star is merely a hope, with the implication that to less hollow men it would be a conviction of faith. Biographically it may be of interest that Eliot in 1925 presented the two senses simultaneously. Critically it must be held a defect that such a clash of sense is left unresolved; instead of complex balance we have, once we notice the ambiguity, an uneasy see-saw from one simple meaning to the opposite. Such a thing is rare if not unique in Eliot's poetry.

More usually a grammatical ambiguity gives compression and complexity. Matthiessen notes an early example, where only compression is secured:

> . . . the violet hour, the evening hour that strives
> Homeward, and brings the sailor home from sea,
> The typist home at teatime, clears her breakfast, lights
> Her stove, and lays out food in tins.

In later poems subtler purposes are served by giving a double grammatical function to a phrase, or telescoping two grammatical structures into one. The first section of 'Ash-Wednesday' merges line after line into an almost unpunctuated series of sentences with clauses that may be equally the end of one sentence or the beginning of the next. For instance, we may take as one statement the four lines

> And I pray that I may forget
> These matters that with myself I too much discuss
> Too much explain
> Because I do not hope to turn again

Or we can take the fourth line as the beginning of another statement:

> Because I do not hope to turn again
> Let these words answer
> For what is done, not to be done again

And this last line opens another sentence:

> For what is done, not to be done again
> May the judgement not be too heavy upon us.

The structure allows a constant overlapping of one unit of sense with another, all mutually consistent though expressing different aspects of the poet's attitude to his situation. Here and in 'Ash-Wednesday' as a whole the effect is to convey not a succession of related attitudes but a fusion which is slightly different from them all: resignation, contrition, suffering and patience (where ordinary usage has had to make two concepts out of synonyms), intense weariness and awareness of strength remaining, hope of forgiveness, longing to regress and longing for a new start which is still the same journey continued. The poem defines a complex attitude for which we have no name, although nameable attitudes form the boundaries within which it has been created.

Perhaps the grammatical ambiguity which is one of the means contributing to the achievement should be treated as an aspect of what I called the third kind of obscurity, that arising more generally from the complexity of what has to be said and from the difficult task of *not* saying something rather like it and more familiar. In parts of the later poems Eliot's 'meaning', what he intends his words to do, is so complex and difficult that direct explicit statement is ruled out. Much of 'Burnt Norton', for instance, is not using current concepts to make a statement, not even a subtle statement. Instead, it is exploring possibilities of meaning that lurk in the interstices of familiar ideas.

Ordinarily our abstract ideas are over-comprehensive and include too wide a range of feeling to be of much use by themselves. If our words 'regret' and 'eternity' were exact bits of mosaic with which to build patterns much of 'Burnt Norton' would not have had to be written. But

> . . . Words strain,
> Crack and sometimes break, under the burden,
> Under the tension, slip, slide, perish,
> Decay with imprecision, will not stay in place,
> Will not stay still.

One could say, perhaps, that the poem takes the place of
the ideas of 'regret' and 'eternity'. Where in ordinary
speech we should have to use those words, and hope by
conversational trial-and-error to obviate the grosser misunderstandings, this poem is a newly created concept,
equally abstract but vastly more exact and rich in meaning.
It makes no statement. It is no more 'about' anything than
an abstract term like 'love' is about anything: it is a
linguistic creation. And the creation of a new concept,
with all the assimilation and communication of experience
that that involves, is perhaps the greatest of linguistic
achievements.

In this poem the new meaning is approached by two
methods. The first is the presentation of concrete images
and definite events, each of which is checked and passes
over into another before it has developed far enough to
stand meaningfully by itself. This is, of course, an extension of a familiar language process. If you try to observe
introspectively how the meaning of an abstract term—
say 'trade'—exists in your mind, you find that after a
moment of blankness, in which there seems to be only
imageless 'meaning', concrete images of objects and events
begin to occur to you; but none by itself carries the full
meaning of the word 'trade', and each is faded out and
replaced by another. The abstract concept, in fact, seems
like a space surrounded and defined by a more or less rich
collection of latent ideas. It is this kind of definition that
Eliot sets about here—in the magnificent first section for

instance—with every subtlety of verbal and rhythmical suggestion.

And the complementary method is to make pseudo-statements in highly abstract language, for the purpose, essentially, of putting forward and immediately rejecting ready-made concepts that might have seemed to approximate to the concept he is creating. For instance:

> Neither from nor towards; at the still point, there the dance is,
> But neither arrest nor movement. And do not call it fixity.
> Where past and future are gathered. Neither movement from
> nor towards,
> Neither ascent nor decline.

Or

> Not the stillness of the violin, while the note lasts,
> Not that only, but the co-existence,
> Or say that the end precedes the beginning,
> And the end and the beginning were always there
> Before the beginning and after the end.
> And all is always now.

In neither of these methods is there any attempt to state the meaning by taking existing abstract ideas and piecing them together in the ordinary way. Where something approaching this more usual method is attempted the result is a little less interesting; for instance

> The inner freedom from the practical desire,
> The release from action and suffering, release from the inner
> And the outer compulsion, yet surrounded
> By a grace of sense, a white light still and moving,
> *Erhebung* without motion, concentration
> Without elimination, both a new world
> And the old made explicit, understood
> In the completion of its partial ecstasy,
> The resolution of its partial horror.

There, abstract concepts already available are being used,

for an individual purpose, it is true, but tending towards generalization away from, rather than through, particularities of experience.

The more characteristic method shows up clearly if we contrast the later Wordsworth and the later Eliot on themes not totally unlike:

> Those fervent raptures have for ever flown;
> And since that date, my soul hath undergone
> Change manifold, for better or for worse:
> Yet cease I not to struggle, and aspire
> Heavenward; and chide the part of me that flags,
> Through sinful choice; or dread necessity
> On human nature from above imposed.
>
> ('The Excursion,' Book IV)
>
> Distraction, music of the flute, stops and steps of the mind
>   over the third stair,
> Fading, fading; strength beyond hope and despair
> Climbing the third stair.
>
> ('Ash Wednesday', III)
>
> Wavering between the profit and the loss
> In this brief transit where the dreams cross
> The dreamcrossed twilight between birth and dying
> (Bless me father) though I do not wish to wish these things
> From the wide window towards the granite shore
> The white sails still fly seaward flying
> Unbroken wings.
>
> And the lost heart stiffens and rejoices
> In the lost lilac and the lost sea voices
>
> ('Ash Wednesday', VI)

In the Wordsworth passage the intensity of experience is diluted in the process of being extended into a general statement. Eliot's statement has equally general application, is equally abstract. But the abstraction is conveyed in writing that half reveals, and half brushes aside, vividly concrete experiences, incidents and occasions, all of which have force and vitality in their own right. Leavis sums it up when he says (*Scrutiny*, XI, 1; Summer 1942), 'his poetry is remarkable for the extraordinary force, penetration and stamina with which it makes its explorations into the concrete actualities of experience below the conceptual currency'.

7

The Changed Outlook in Eliot's Later Poems

THE impact of Eliot's poetry when it appeared was in-evitably something different from its effect now when we go back to it without the context of its time. The later assessments may be juster, and will inevitably be different, but the earlier perhaps have their interest and their historical claim. For that reason I risk reproducing four brief inquiries, all tied closely to their time and circumstances but related to one another by their reference to changes not only in the poetry but in the audience it met. The first is a review (Scrutiny, III, 2; September 1934) of The Rock, Book of Words, 1934.

'The view that what we need in this tempestuous turmoil of change is a Rock to shelter under or to cling to, rather than an efficient aeroplane in which to ride it, is comprehensible but mistaken.' The attitude by Dr I. A. Richards here is one that many people now find less alluring than once they did, and to them the general theme of *The Rock* will be welcome. The whole book bears witness to the conviction that the only possible advance at the present time is a 'spiritual' one and has little to do with anything specifically modern, nor any appeal for those who

> . . . constantly try to escape
> From the darkness outside and within
> By dreaming of systems so perfect that no one will need to be
>   good.

Mr Eliot's subtle tone of humble and yet militant contempt could hardly be improved upon. What is not convincing, however, is his suggestion that the Church is the only alternative, for his pleading relies upon false antitheses. It puts the plight of the uncultured vividly, but it does not show what the Church would do for them. A description of the breakdown of social and particularly of family life ends

> But every son would have his motor cycle,
> And daughters ride away on casual pillions.

But the alternative to the pillion is not suggested. As far as we can judge from the time when such families were more stable, it would be the horsehair sofa, in a front parlour left vacant by the rest of the family with appropriate pleasantries. The only alternative to godless restlessness that this book gives are the rough diamond piety of the builder's foreman and, more impressive, the satisfactions of the highly cultured who happen to be within the Church:

> Shall we not bring to Your service all our powers
> For life, for dignity, grace and order,
> And intellectual pleasures of the senses?

But the plight of people capable of appreciating such culture and still outside the Church is not put. In so far as *The Rock* is pleading for certain attitudes which the Church at its best supports it is undoubtedly effective, as it equally is in its denunciatory description of things as they are, of the misery of the poor and the spiritual vacuity of the well-to-do. It is in the choruses where these descriptions occur that the greatest intrinsic value of the work is to be found.

The prose dialogue which maintains the action of the pageant is distressing. It is difficult to believe that the spinsterish Cockney of the builders was written by the author of the public house scene in *The Waste Land*, and the speeches of the Agitator and the fashionable visitors to the Church are just the usual middle-class caricatures of a reality that has never been accurately observed. They are the caricatures of a class by a class, and well worn and blurred they are, inevitably. The reach-me-down character of the dialogue is partly responsible for and partly derived from—in fact is one with—the banal and sentimental treatment of a scene like The Crusaders' Farewell, which offers so painful a contrast to the dignity of the liturgical Latin that comes next. Only in some of the ingenious pastiches of archaic styles which Mr Eliot introduces from time to time is the prose readable with even mild pleasure.

The verse is altogether more interesting. Naturally in a work written to order and presumably in a limited time there is included some which is not as fine as most of what Mr Eliot has published. Necessarily, too, this verse cannot have the concentration and subtlety of a short poem intended for many attentive readings. Its interest lies rather in its experimentation with a tone of address. Innovations of 'tone' (in Richards' sense) are at least as significant as innovations of 'technique' in the restricted sense, and in the addresses of the Chorus and The Rock to the decent heathen and the ineffectual devout, who are taken as forming the audience, Mr Eliot achieves a tone that is new to contemporary verse. Its peculiar kind of sermonizing is especially welcome in contrast to the kind the young communist poets offer us: in particular it succeeds in upbraiding those it addresses while still remaining humble and *impersonally* superior to them:

> The Word of the Lord came unto me, saying:
> O miserable cities of designing men,
> O wretched generation of enlightened men,
>
> .   .   .   .   .
>
> Will you build me a house of plaster, with corrugated roofing,
> To be filled with a litter of Sunday newspapers?

And again:

> Do you need to be told that even such modest attainments
> As you can boast in the way of polite society
> Will hardly survive the Faith to which they owe their
> significance?

Just occasionally the tone verges on the sententious:

> The lot of man is ceaseless labour,
> Or ceaseless idleness, which is still harder . . .

but usually its poise is perfect.

Closely bound up with the tone of address is the texture of the language. The idiom Mr Eliot has developed here is admirably suited to, and has evidently emerged from pressure of, the practical circumstances of the work: its dramatic presentation before an audience whose muzzy respect for the devotional had to be welded to a concern for contemporary realities. A particularly successful and characteristic trick of idiom is the quick transition from vaguely Biblical language to the contemporary colloquial. It can be seen in this:

> I have trodden the wine-press alone, and I know
> That it is hard to be really useful

and in this:

> And they write innumerable books; being too vain and dis-
> tracted for silence; seeking every one after his own eleva-
> tion, and dodging his emptiness.

This passage also illustrates the dominant feeling of the denunciatory choruses, a dry contempt which has passed beyond the stage of tiredness and now has a tough springiness:

> O weariness of men who turn from God
> To the grandeur of your mind and the glory of your action,
>
> .   .   .   .   .
>
> Engaged in devising the perfect refrigerator,

Engaged in working out a rational morality,
Engaged in printing as many books as possible,
Plotting of happiness and flinging empty bottles,
Turning from your vacancy to fevered enthusiasm
For nation or race or what you call humanity; . . .

The Rock is in many ways typical of Mr Eliot's later work. Far less concentrated, far less perfect, far more easy-going than the earlier work, it has an increased breadth of contact with the world which takes the place of intensity of contact at a few typical points. The change is not one that can be described briefly. It can be roughly indicated by saying that the earlier work seemed to be produced by the ideal type of a generation, and asked for Mr Eliot to be looked upon almost as an institution, whereas this later work, though not more individual, is far more personal. What seems certain is that it forms a transition to a stage of Mr Eliot's work which has not yet fully defined itself.

*   *   *   *   *

The change of outlook was still more evident in Collected Poems 1909-1935, *which I discussed in* Scrutiny, *V*, 2; *September* 1936.

This new volume is an opportunity, not for a review—for 'The Poetry of T. S. Eliot' begins to have the intimidating sound of a Tripos question—but for asking whether anything in the development of the poetry accounts for the change in attitude that has made Mr Eliot's work less *chic* now than it was ten years ago. Perhaps the ten years are a sufficient explanation—obvious changes in fashionable feeling have helped to make the sort-of-communist poets popular. But on the other hand it may be that these poets gratify some taste that Mr Eliot also gratified in his earlier work but not in his later. If so it is surely a taste

for evocations of the sense of protest that our circumstances set up in us; for it seems likely that at the present
time it is expressions of protest in some form or other that
most readily gain a poet popular sympathy. And up to
The Waste Land and *The Hollow Men* this protest—
whether distressed, disgusted or ironical—was still the
dominant note of Mr Eliot's work, through all the
subtlety and sensitiveness of the forms it took. Yet already
in these two poems the suggestion was creeping in that
the sufferers were also failures. We are the hollow men,
but there are, besides,

> Those who have crossed
> With direct eyes, to death's other Kingdom

And in all the later work the stress tends to fall on the
regret or suffering that arises from our own choices or our
inherent limitations, or on the resignation that they make
necessary. Without at the moment trying to define the
change more closely one can point out certain characteristics of the later work which are likely to displease those
who create the fashions of taste in poetry today, and which
also contrast with Mr Eliot's earlier work. First it is true
that in some of the poems (most obviously in the Choruses
from *The Rock*) there are denunciation and preaching,
both of which people like just now. But there is a vital
difference between the denunciation here and that, say, in
The Dog Beneath the Skin: Mr Eliot doesn't invite you to
step across a dividing line and join him in guaranteed
rightness—he suggests at the most that you and he should
both try, in familiar and difficult ways, not to live so
badly. Failing to make it sound easy, and not putting
much stress on the fellowship of the just, he offers no
satisfaction to the craving for a life that is ethically and
emotionally *simpler*.

And this characteristic goes with a deeper change of

attitude that separates the later work from the earlier. Besides displaying little faith in a revolt against anything outside himself, Mr Eliot in his recent work never invites you to believe that everything undesirable in you is due to outside influences that can be blamed for tampering with your original rightness. Not even in the perhaps over-simple 'Animula' is there any suggestion that the 'simple soul' has suffered an avoidable wrong for which someone else can be given the blame. Mr Eliot declines to sanction an implicit belief, almost universally held, which lies behind an immense amount of rationalization, self-pity and childish protest—the belief that the very fact of being alive ought to ensure your being a satisfactory object in your own sight. He is nearer the more rational view that the process of living is at its best one of progressive dissatisfaction.

Throughout the earlier poems there are traces of what, if it were cruder and without irony and impersonality, would be felt at once as self-pity or futile protest: for example,

> Put your shoes at the door, sleep, prepare for life.
> The last twist of the knife.

or,

> Wipe your hand across your mouth, and laugh;
> The worlds revolve like ancient women
> Gathering fuel in vacant lots.

or again,

> The nightingales are singing near
> The Convent of the Sacred Heart,
>
> And sang within the bloody wood
> When Agamemnon cried aloud,
> And let their liquid siftings fall
> To stain the stiff dishonoured shroud.

Obviously this is only one aspect of the early poetry, and to lay much stress on it without qualification would be grotesquely unfair to 'Gerontion' especially, and to other poems of that phase. But it is a prominent enough aspect of the work to have made critics, one might have thought, more liable to underrate the earlier poems than, with fashionable taste, the later ones. For there can be no doubt of the greater maturity of feeling in the later work:

> And I pray that I may forget
> These matters that with myself I too much discuss
> Too much explain
> Because I do not hope to turn again
> Let these words answer
> For what is done, not to be done again
> May the judgment not be too heavy upon us

This may be called religious submission, but essentially it is the submission of maturity.

What is peculiar to Mr Eliot in the tone of his work, and not inherent in maturity or in religion, is that he does *submit* to what he knows rather than welcome it. To say that his is a depressed poetry isn't true, because of the extraordinary toughness and resilience that always underlie it. They show, for instance, in the quality of the scorn he expresses for those who have tried to overlook what he sees:

> . . . the strained time-ridden faces
> Distracted from distraction by distraction
> Filled with fancies and empty of meaning
> Tumid apathy with no concentration
> Men and bits of paper . . .

But to insist on the depression yields a half-truth. For though acceptance and understanding have taken the place of protest the underlying experience remains one of suffering, and the renunciation is much more vividly communicated than the advance for the sake of which it was made. It is summed up in the ending of 'Ash-Wednesday':

> Blessèd sister, holy mother, spirit of the fountain, spirit of the
>   garden,
> Suffer us not to mock ourselves with falsehood
> Teach us to care and not to care
> Teach us to sit still
> Even among these rocks,
> Our peace in His will
> And even among these rocks
> Sister, mother
> And spirit of the river, spirit of the sea,
> Suffer me not to be separated
>
> And let my cry come unto Thee.

This is the cry of the weaned child, I suppose the analysts might say; and without acquiescing in the developmental view they would imply one can agree that weaning stands as a type-experience of much that Mr Eliot is interested in as a poet. It seems to be the clearer and more direct realization of this kind of experience that makes the later poems at the same time more personal and more mature. And in the presence of these poems many who liked saying they liked the earlier work feel both embarrassed and snubbed.

*　　　*　　　*　　　*　　　*

F. R. Leavis, in a sensitively accurate and concentrated study of Eliot's later poetry (Scrutiny, XI, 1, Summer 1942), took his account up to 'The Dry Salvages' which had just appeared, and gave me the opportunity six months later (Scrutiny, XI, 3; Spring 1943) of writing about the last of the 'Four Quartets', 'Little Gidding'. As he had remarked, 'The Dry Salvages', continuing the new start begun in 'Burnt Norton', is 'preoccupied with the nature of acceptance and belief'.

The opening of 'Little Gidding' speaks of renewed life of unimaginable splendour, seen in promise amidst the cold decline of age. It offers no revival of life-processes; it is a spring time, 'But not in time's covenant'. If this 'midwinter spring' has such blooms as the snow on hedges,

> Where is the summer, the unimaginable
> Zero summer?

With the sun blazing on the ice, the idea of pentecostal fire, of central importance in the poem, comes in for the first time, an intense, blinding promise of life and (as later passages show) almost unbearable.

The church of Little Gidding introduces another theme of the poem. Anchored in time and space, but for some people serving as the world's end where they can fulfil a purpose outside time and space, it gives contact with spiritual concerns through earthly and human things.

A third theme, important for the whole poem, is also stated in the first section: that the present is able to take up, and even give added meaning to, the values of the past. Here too the pentecostal idea comes in:

> And what the dead had no speech for, when living,
> They can tell you, being dead: the communication
> Of the dead is tongued with fire beyond the language of the
> living.

Section II can be regarded as the *logical* starting point of the whole poem. It deals with the desolation of death and the futility of life for those who have had no conviction of spiritual values in their life's work. First come three sharply organized riming stanzas to evoke, by image and idea but without literal statement, our sense of the hopeless death of air, earth, fire and water, seen not only as the elements of man's existence but as the means of his destruction and dismissal. The tone having been set by these stanzas, there opens a narrative passage describing the dreary bitterness in which a life of literary culture can end if it has brought no sense of spiritual values. The life presented is one, such as Mr Eliot's own, of effort after clear speech and exact thought, and the passage amounts to a shuddering 'There but for the grace of God go I'. It reveals more clearly than ever the articles in *The Criterion* did, years ago, what it was in 'humanism' that Mr Eliot recoiled from so violently. What the humanist's ghost sees in his life are futility, isolation, and guilt on account of his self-assertive prowess—'Which once you took for exercise of virtue'—and the measure of aggression against others which that must bring.

The verse in this narrative passage, with its regular measure and insistent alliteration, so effective for combining the macabre with the urbane and dreary, is a way to indicate and a way to control the pressure of urgent misery and self-disgust. The motive power of this passage, as of so much of Mr Eliot's earlier poetry, is repulsion. But in the poem as a whole, the other motive force is dominant: there is a movement of feeling and conviction outwards, reaching towards what attracts. The other parts of the poem can be viewed as working out an alternative to the prospect of life presented in this narrative.

Section III sees the foundation for such an alternative in the contact with spiritual values, especially as they appear in the tradition of the past. Detachment (distinguished from indifference) allows us to use both our own past and the historical past in such a way as to draw on their present spiritual significance for us without entangling us in regressive yearning for a pattern which no longer is:

> History may be servitude,
> History may be freedom. See, now they vanish.
> The faces and places, with the self which, as it could, loved
>   them,
> To become renewed, transfigured, in another pattern.

Once we accept the significance of the spiritual motives and intentions of the past, even the factions connected with the church and community of Little Gidding leave us an inheritance; we can be at one with the whole past, including the sinning and defeated past, for its people were spiritually alive,

> All touched by common genius,
> United in the strife which divided them.

But the humanist's fate cannot be escaped in so gentle and placid a way; a more formidable ordeal is waiting. In contrast to the leisurely meditation of section III, the fourth section is a forceful passage, close-knit with rime and incisive. Its theme is the terrifying fierceness of the pentecostal experience, the dove bringing fire. This is not the fire of expiation, such as the humanist had to suffer. It is the consuming experience of love, the surrender to a spiritual principle beyond us, and the only alternative to consuming ourselves with the miserable fires of sin and error. This pentecostal ordeal must be met before the blinding promise seen in 'midwinter spring' can be accepted.

The final section develops the idea that every experience is integrated with all the others, so that the fulness of exploration means a return, with better understanding, to the point where you started. The theme has already been foreshadowed in section III where detachment is seen to give liberation from the future as well as the past, so that neither past nor future has any fascination of a kind that could breed in us a reluctance to accept the present fully.

The tyranny of sequence and duration in life is thus reduced. Time-processes are viewed as aspects of a pattern which can be grasped in its entirety at any one of its moments:

> The moment of the rose and the moment of the yew-tree
> Are of equal duration.

One effect of this view of time and experience is to rob the moment of death of any over-significance we may have given it. For the humanist of section II life trails off just because it can't manage to endure. For the man convinced of spiritual values life is a coherent pattern in which the ending has its due place, and, because it is part of a pattern, itself leads into the beginning. An over-strong terror of death is often one expression of the fear of living, for death is one of the life-processes that seem too terrifying to be borne. In examining one means of becoming reconciled to death, Mr Eliot can show us life too made bearable, unfrightening, postively inviting:

> With the drawing of this Love and the voice of this Calling
> We shall not cease from exploration
> And the end of all our exploring
> Will be to arrive where we started
> And know the place for the first time.

Here is the clearest expression of a motive force other than repulsion. Its dominance makes this poem—to put it very simply—far happier than most of Mr Eliot's.

Being reconciled to death and the conditions of life restores the golden age of unfearful natural living and lets you safely, without regression, recapture the wonder and easy rightness of certain moments, especially in early childhood:

> At the source of the longest river
> The voice of the hidden waterfall
> And the children in the apple-tree
> Not known, because not looked for
> But heard, half-heard, in the stillness
> Between two waves of the sea.
> Quick now, here, now, always—
> A condition of complete simplicity
> (Costing not less than everything)

The whole of this last section suggests a serene and revitalized return from meditation to one's part in active living. It includes a re-affirmation of that concern with speech which has made up so much of Mr Eliot's work and which could have been the bitter futility that it is for the ghostly humanist. The re-affirming passage (introduced as a simile to suggest the integrated patterning of all living experience) is an example of amazing condensation, of most comprehensive thinking given the air of leisured speech—not conversation but the considered speech of a man talking to a small group who are going to listen for a time without replying. It is one example of the intellectual quality of this poem. In most of Mr Eliot's poems the intellectual materials which abound are used emotionally. In much of this poem they are used intellectually, in literal statement which is to be understood literally (for instance, the opening of section III). How such statements become poetry is a question outside the range of this review. To my mind they do, triumphantly, and for me it ranks among the major good fortunes of our time that so superb a poet is writing.

*   *   *   *   *

Ten years later, at the British Council Summer School in Oxford, 1953, I tried to be more explicit about the change from the earlier to the later poems.

Superficially it might be called a change from bitterness to more meditative tranquillity, and from images of desolation to images of life appreciated. The later work, often Christian in idiom, is of course welcomed by Christian commentators and disliked by some of Eliot's earlier readers (see, e.g., R. N. Higinbotham, in *Scrutiny*, XI, 4; Summer 1943).

'Perch'Io Non Spero', the first poem in the 'Ash-

Wednesday' sequence, appeared in 1928, three years after 'The Hollow Men', and is the first clear statement of a decisively changed outlook. According to Helen Gardner (*The Art of T. S. Eliot*, London, 1949), the first line, 'Because I do not hope to turn again' , is adapted from 'the opening line of a poem by Cavalcanti, written when he was dying in exile and had no hope of ever returning to Tuscany and to his lady'. Thus there is implied a recognition of the impossibility of going back over your steps:

> Because I do not hope to know again
> The infirm glory of the positive hour
> Because I do not think
> Because I know I shall not know
> The one veritable transitory power
> Because I cannot drink
> There, where trees flower, and springs
>   flow, for there is nothing again

Where is it, then, that trees flower and springs flow? Evidently in the past that the poet cannot re-live. But the past of this poet was characteristically 'The Waste Land'; and it seems therefore that something very remarkable has happened.

It means, as I understand it, a tremendous change of attitude, one in which the experience of 'The Waste Land' is revalued, with much more emphasis on the fact that the disillusionment and dreariness we suffer there are in part self-inflicted. Our defeat is possible only because of our own contributory failure. That seems already to have been implied by the reference to *The Heart of Darkness* in 'The Hollow Men', and Helen Gardner (whose excellent analysis of that poem seems to me the best part of her book) has selected the relevant passage from Conrad's story. 'There was something wanting in him,' writes Conrad of his character Kurtz who was defeated by the wilderness of the tropical jungle, 'some small matter which, when the pressing need arose, could not be found under his magnificent eloquence. Whether he knew of this deficiency himself I can't say. I think the knowledge came to him at last—only at the very last. But the wilderness had found him out early, and had taken on him a terrible vengeance for the fantastic invasion. I think it had whispered to him things about himself which he did not know, things of which he had no conception till he took counsel with this great solitude—and the whisper had proved irresistibly fascinating. It echoed loudly within him because he was hollow at the core.'

The poem does, however, indicate a contrast to the hollow men. There are also

> Those who have crossed
> With direct eyes, to death's other kingdom

and it is they who remember the rest of us

>   . . . only
> As the hollow men
> The stuffed men.

The contrast, the implication that there is an alternative, is sometimes overlooked.

The later poems would hardly be conceivable in the absence of earlier hints of the view that disappointment and disgust with living experience are in some degree the result of one's own failure. Self-blame and self-contempt have a very definite place, for instance in 'Prufrock', 'Portrait of a Lady' and 'Gerontion'. And the sense of the present as the smoky candle-end of time—an heroic age grown shabby, a golden age turned pinchbeck—is accompanied by hints that we have only our illusions to blame for our disappointments. In 'A Cooking Egg'

> Where are the eagles and the trumpets?

may seem a lament for the lost heroic age, until we remember that it stands in parallel with

> But where is the penny world I bought . . .?

The implication is that the age of the eagles and the trumpets was no more what we would have liked it to be than the cooking egg was the new-laid egg at a bargain price that the boy had hoped. As if the implication is not clear enough in 'A Cooking Egg', it is made explicit later on in 'Triumphal March', where the crowd that gapes and perceives nothing is made to say, when the procession has passed,

> That is all we could see. But how many
> eagles! and how many trumpets!

—and this crowd that has got its eagles and trumpets is exactly the spiritually dead crowd that Eliot denounces in *The Rock*.

Even the disillusionment with sexual love is seen against a hinted contrast in 'The Waste Land', a possibility not realized. At the beginning there is the hyacinth girl:

> —Yet when we came back, late, from the Hyacinth garden,
> Your arms full, and your hair wet, I could not
> Speak, and my eyes failed, I was neither
> Living nor dead, and I knew nothing,
> Looking into the heart of light, the silence.

At the end there are the three positives, Give, Sympathise, Control, and the passage on 'control' is specially interesting:

> The boat responded
> Gaily, to the hand expert with sail and oar
> The sea was calm, your heart would have responded
> Gaily, when invited, beating obedient
> To controlling hands.

Not only is the word 'gaily' used, a reference to a mood almost completely missing from the poems, but the tense is significant: 'Your heart would have responded'. Speaking of what might have been is very different from repining at the stale and disappointing quality of things.

Attitudes of disillusionment and protest have no expression after 'The Hollow Men'. It is the alternative, the might have been, that provides the recurrent theme. The position revealed in the later work has some affinity with Donne's in Holy Sonnet III (discussed more fully in the first essay):

> That sufferance was my sinne; now I repent;
> 'Cause I did suffer, I must suffer paine . . .
> . . . for long, yet vehement griefe hath beene
> Th'effect and cause, the punishment and sinne.

The mood of self-reproach is fairly prominent, as Helen Gardner has shown, in 'The Hollow Men'. Later, in 'Ash-Wednesday', we find the much more effective tension between two directions of desire. The first is that of going on positively to something unknown:

> Consequently I rejoice, having to construct something
> Upon which to rejoice.

The second is the regret for the lost satisfactions of earlier life, lost in the double sense of being now out of reach and of not having been fully enjoyed when they might have been.

The sense of what might have been, of loss and of recognized possibility, is contemplated more fully in the 'Four Quartets':

> What might have been is an abstraction
> Remaining a perpetual possibility
> Only in a world of speculation.

In one aspect the 'Four Quartets' can be seen as an effort

to find some way in which the unlived past can be subsumed in the life of the present:

> Time past and time future
> What might have been and what has been
> Point to one end, which is always present.

As in Donne and Hardy ('Yet we were looking away') there is a sense of having missed something that past experience should have yielded; but in Eliot there is also the resilient determination to find it somehow in the present:

> The moments of happiness—not the sense of well-being,
> Fruition, fulfilment, security or affection,
> Or even a very good dinner, but the sudden illumination—
> We had the experience but missed the meaning,
> And approach to the meaning restores the experience
> In a different form, beyond any meaning
> We can assign to happiness.

In their subtle examination of the significance of time for human values, the 'Four Quartets' begin and end with an insistence on the present—

> Quick now, here, now always

—with the capacity of the present moment for implying the whole of life and so freeing us from the waste and uncertainty of time. The last section of 'Little Gidding' enlarges on and confirms the words with which 'Burnt Norton' ends:

> Sudden in a shaft of sunlight
> Even while the dust moves
> There rises the hidden laughter
> Of children in the foliage
> Quick now, here, now, always—
> Ridiculous the waste sad time
> Stretching before and after.

If we believe that the later poems mark a great advance even on the remarkable achievement of the earlier we have to be on guard against regarding the earlier as in some way superseded, interesting only as a stage of development. Apart from their extraordinary effectiveness as arrangements of words, they present in theme and mood important and recurrent possibilities of experience. If their protest, distaste, ironic detachment are in some degree immature, they are also deeply entrenched as possibilities for sensitive people in our culture.

At the end of such an essay as this, it may seem belated to quote Leavis on the danger of substituting elucidation for criticism: 'There is a clear tendency to frustrate the enormous labour expended by the poet in undercutting mere acceptance, inhibiting inert acquiescence, and circumventing, at every level, what may be called *cliché*; a tendency, that is, to abet the reader's desire to arrive without having travelled' (*Scrutiny*, XV, 1; December 1947). To enjoy poetry and assess its worth to us, we have to maintain the difficult balance that Eliot himself has described: 'On the one hand the critic may busy himself so much with the implications of a poem, or of one poet's work—implications moral, social, religious or other— that the poetry becomes barely more than a text for a discourse. . . . Or if you stick too closely to the "poetry" and adopt no attitude towards what the poet has to say, you will tend to evacuate it of all significance' (*The Use of Poetry and the Use of Criticism*, London, 1933).

8

Progression of Theme in Eliot's Modern Plays[1]

AS a result of Eliot's widened popularity and heightened public repute in recent times, accompanied as they are by a persistent undercurrent of the antagonism he used to provoke, we can expect a tide of adverse criticism to flow against him with growing force over the next few years. It will largely be due to the psychological processes that govern vogue, its causal connection with the merits and limitations of his work being tenuous and indirect. Although, no doubt, Eliot's literary criticism will soon come under fire, the most inviting targets for the first attacks have been the plays. In this situation the place of criticism—discriminating assessment—is only too likely to be usurped by the confident reversal of attitude that comes from lackeying the varying tide.

As a first step towards assessment we need to be clear what the plays are about and what Eliot has done in them. Comments on the quality of characterization, the dramatic structure, the verse form or any other of the conventional foci of critical attention are beside the point unless we are clear about the interests and attitudes that the plays convey. In the course of saying what statements the plays seem to make a critical evaluation may begin to emerge, but my aim is only elucidation; and the misconceptions evident in some of the critics' comments suggest that the task is not altogether easy, nor a waste of time.

[1] Based on the Wood Memorial Lecture given at Hughes Hall, Cambridge, England, 21 May 1955.

In Eliot's plays a theme that has appeared in many of his poems is taken further and handled more explicitly: the theme of separation. It is associated in the poems with what can loosely be called a mother-figure—a woman in the role of protector, guide, guardian, intercessor—but it goes beyond that into the Christian idea of longing to be at one with God by overcoming separation from him. In the passage from *Ash-Wednesday* quoted in the preceding essay the two themes are fused:

> Even among these rocks,
> Our peace in His will
> And even among these rocks
> Sister, mother
> And spirit of the river, spirit of the sea,
> Suffer me not to be separated
>
> And let my cry come unto Thee.

Though the last lines come from Christian prayers, they are fused here with the image of a woman.

In *Difficulties of a Statesman*, the protest against insurmountable difficulties and inextricable confusions in public affairs works up to a broken cry for peace and quiet and union with the mother:

> O mother (not among these busts, all correctly inscribed)
> I a tired head among these heads
> Necks strong to bear them
> Noses strong to break the wind
> Mother
> May we not be some time, almost now, together,
> If the mactations, immolations, oblations, impetrations,
> Are now observed
> May we not be
> O hidden
> Hidden in the stillness of noon, in the silent croaking night.

Part of the interest of the plays lies in their having provided a method of treating problems of actual experience—a method midway between the direct statement of personal experience (which Eliot makes a point of avoiding) and the digestion of experience into abstract contemplation and remote symbol as in the Quartets. They therefore give him, among other things, release from the exceedingly intensive working of a small range of symbols.

*　　*　　*　　*　　*

The Family Reunion offers a very direct treatment of the separation experience called by Ian Suttie and other psycho-therapists 'psychological weaning': that is, the psychological separation of mother and child which, in fortunate circumstances carried out willingly by both of them, leaves them individual social beings, independent but not isolated. Everyone knows that this process may meet difficulties, often due to the mother's reluctance (perhaps unconscious) to let go of the child, especially if the intimate companionships of her own life have not been satisfying. Much of Eliot's work implies the importance of this problem when it persists into adult life and the importance of related problems with which it resonates psychologically.

But we have to resist any temptation to regard these parts of his work as 'just' the expression of separation anxiety. It would be an error—one not always avoided by the earlier psychoanalysts—to imply that when a thread of related experiences is traced back to infantile forms the significance of the adult forms is necessarily reduced. The truth is that the early events sometimes give rise in vivid, simple, unmistakable form to experiences that go on all through life and constitute an inescapable part of human experience. Separation anxiety is one form of the experience of loneliness that accompanies the definition of individuality. We must be capable of tolerating it in some degree if we are to be true to the unique person that each of us potentially is. But at the same time we want community. Tension inevitably arises for the individual in society, in that he wants to be both truly individual and truly in community.

Many anodynes have been tried for the pain of this form of loneliness: alcohol is one, political addictions another. In religious thought the experience has been related to the idea of the individual's longing for union with God and striving towards that even at the cost of relinquishing human companionship. For Eliot this has been a highly significant theme. As epigraph to *Sweeney Agonistes* he took the words from St John of the Cross: 'Hence the soul cannot be possessed of the divine union, until it has divested itself of the love of created beings.' In *The Rock* he writes:

> What life have you if you have not life together?
> There is no life that is not in community,
> And no community not lived in praise of God,
> Even the anchorite who meditates alone,
> For whom the days and nights repeat the praise of God,
> Prays for the Church, the Body of Christ incarnate.

And in *Murder in the Cathedral* the worst evil of hell is

> Emptiness, absence, separation from God.

*   *   *   *   ·   *

In *The Family Reunion*, however, he deals directly with the problem of individual separation from the mother, as well as the theme of a religious conversion. The hero, Harry, returns home to a dominating mother who has never agreed to letting go of him or any of her family, apart from discarding the husband with whom she was totally unhappy:

> I keep Wishwood alive
> To keep the family alive, to keep them together,
> To keep me alive, and I live to keep them.

The ambiguity of the last phrase admirably conveys the confusion of emotional dependence.

Harry is tormented by the death-wish that he harboured against his wife, his marriage having been a failure and ending with his wife's being lost from a ship in the Atlantic. He is under the same curse as his father and mother were in their loveless marriage, and he is hounded down by the pursuing Furies for his death-wish—this violent reaction against the woman to whom he was tied being, of course, entirely different from real independence of the mother-figure, which he has never achieved.

The return homes intensifies his sense both of being under a curse and also of his mother's domination and emotional dependence:

> Everything has always been referred back to mother.
> When we were children, before we went to school,
> The rule of conduct was simply pleasing mother;
> Misconduct was simply being unkind to mother;
> What was wrong was whatever made her suffer,
> And whatever made her happy was what was virtuous—
> Though never very happy, I remember. That was why
> We all felt like failures, before we had begun.
> When we came back, for the school holidays,
> They were not holidays, but simply a time
> In which we were supposed to make up to mother
> For all the weeks during which she had not seen us . . .

He comes home in a state of exasperated protest against the grappling-irons that these women (mother and wife) have fixed into his life:

>   Family affection
> Was a kind of formal obligation, a duty
> Only noticed by its neglect. One had that part to play.
> After such training, I could endure, these ten years,
> Playing a part that had been imposed upon me;
> And I returned to find another one made ready—

The book laid out, lines underscored, and the costume
Ready to be put on.

His release from his mother comes only when he has heard
the truth about the miserable relations between her and
his father, about the way she had obliterated his father,
and about his father's death-wish against her. With this
knowledge comes his conversion. For one thing, the
futility of the violent death-wish as a substitute for true
independence is made evident by Agatha's account of her
mature reaction to his father's childish plans for murder.
Harry turns away from his former life of emotional over-
dependence, a dependence which he had expressed equally
in accepting imposed roles and in rejecting them with the
infantile violence of exasperation. He turns instead to a
life of chosen and willing love—in him evidently religious
in form—which is totally different from reluctant submission to mutual dependence.

Agatha warns him that the attaining of this mature love
must mean separation from his emotionally-dependent
mother:

> Love compels cruelty
> To those who do not understand love.

He accepts the necessity and leaves his mother, and now
at last he really does kill a woman. The doctor has warned
him that her heart will stand no shock, but he gives her
the worst shock in his power and she goes into the next
room and dies.

Harry's predicament has been a means of uniting
something of the poignancy of partings between a man
and a woman that occurs frequently in the poems (*Portrait
of a Lady*, *La Figlia che Piange*, *Eyes that last I saw in tears*)
with something of the exasperated violence of *Sweeney
Agonistes*:

I knew a man once did a girl in
Any man might do a girl in
Any man has to, needs to, wants to
Once in a life-time, do a girl in.

*   *   *   *   *

This main theme deserves emphasizing (even at the cost of neglecting much else in the play) because it has not been appreciated by some of the better critics, for instance F. O. Matthiessen and Helen Gardner. Mattheissen (*The Achievement of T. S. Eliot*, New York, 1947) regarded the play as a failure. Somehow he failed to see that the break with the mother was a necessary climax, and he makes the hopelessly banal and sentimental comment: 'Hers is the character of blind pride and selfish will that brings on *nemesis*, but Harry's utter lack of compunction seems none the less unnatural.' He was similarly shocked by Harry's feeling no remorse for his death-wish against his wife, an extraordinary point of view since, after all, Harry comes in tortured by remorse. But in his conversion he goes beyond remorse, because his long-delayed separation from his mother at last removes the condition of mind out of which the death-wish grew. In fact Matthiessen's remarks have almost the bewildered, fumbling quality of the comments by the chorus of conventional uncles and aunts. He could not, for instance, accept the possibility of Harry's going off to the wilds or the slums (or wherever he does eventually go) after his life of resorts and luxury hotels; but all such conversions are incredible until they happen, and Matthiessen might just as well find St Francis incredible, or St Paul, or the Buddha.

Helen Gardner (*The Art of T. S. Eliot*, London, 1949) sees more fully into the main theme of the play in so far as it is bound up with Harry's religious conversion, and in concentrating on this she may well be in line with the author's chief conscious intention. But it leads her to do less than justice to the play that he actually wrote. In particular she thinks the effective play has ended before it has. For her the climax is the moment of conversion when Harry realizes that the Furies, instead of hounding him down for his guilt, are waiting now to lead him on the way to expiation and true satisfaction. And so she complains, 'The climax is a dramatic anti-climax. The play ends with Harry's departure and his mother's death. Agatha presumably returns to her college and Mary goes away to take up some kind of career. The single one of these events that can be called dramatic is Amy's death, and the dramatist has to seize on that to round off the play. The true meaning of the play is not, however, in Amy's death, which is merely a consequence, but in Harry's conversion; and that, like Thomas à Becket's sanctity, we have to take for granted. It cannot be expressed in dramatic terms.'

For me the climax is not just the one point, the point of conversion when the Furies appear in their benign form. It spreads more widely; it begins with Harry's understanding of the family situation through his talk with Agatha; this in turn helps him to decide on the compassionate but relentless break with his mother; and then he actually leaves her and so brings about her death. If we must fix on one point as a climax (though I see no good reason why we should) I would choose the parting of Harry and his mother, he to go to his new life, she to turn into the next room and die.

This view of the play's ending also gives an answer to Gardner's other objection, that Harry's conversion cannot be expressed in dramatic terms. For, of course, it can be and is: he expressed it by killing his mother, giving her the sort of shock the doctor had warned him against. This is the dramatic expression of the reality of his conversion and his acceptance of its psychological implications. What precisely he goes to in his future life is rightly left uncertain; it has no place in the extended dramatic moment that constitutes the play.

I find it surprising that Helen Gardner complains of this uncertainty. She says, 'The problem of Mr Eliot's plays arises at their dramatic centre. Their defect, if it is a defect, is a fundamental one; their success, if it is a success, makes it necessary to define again what we mean by drama. We have to ask whether dramatic expressiveness has been achieved if, at the climax of a play, the hero cannot express himself either in action or in words, and the bystander who has the clearest insight can only tell us that what has happened is inexplicable in this world, "the resolution is in another".' Actually what Agatha sees as not to be explained in this world is the general process by which Harry has to expiate the sin of the whole family, and what she treats as being beyond our knowledge and responsibility is the spiritual experience that awaits him. But she is perfectly clear and explicit about what has happened, as she shows when Mary wants her to stop him from going towards the dangers she believes await him. Agatha replies

> Here the danger, here the death, here, not elsewhere;
> Elsewhere no doubt is agony, renunciation,
> But birth and life. Harry has crossed the frontier
> Beyond which safety and danger have a different meaning.
> And he cannot return.

Agatha is clear that what has happened is a psychological birth.

* * * * *

The parting from the mother is one form of the experience of human loneliness. In *The Cocktail Party* the theme is again the loneliness of human beings, with emphasis on the choice they must make of the sort of loneliness and the sort of social communion they will have. The Chamberlaynes' marriage is coming to grief; Celia Coplestone is having an affair with Edward Chamberlayne but early in the play finds that he is not in reality like the fantasy of him that she is in love with; Peter Quilpe is in love with Celia, but he too fails to see her as she is and is in love only with some aspiration of his own. The action of the play shows them coming to understand their problems more clearly, making their choice and living it out. Celia's choice means relinquishing ordinary social life for religious discipline and communion with God through devoted nursing, followed by martyrdom, amongst a remote and primitive people. The Chamberlaynes' choice means that they face the knowledge of their own and each other's difficulty in loving and giving, they make the best of a bad job, and they go on with the conventional social duties represented for them by the cocktail party. Peter at the end of the play reaches the point where he realizes more clearly what sort of choice he has to make, but his story is left untold.

The theme is spread rather thinly over a full-length play and *The Cocktail Party*, lacking the richer complexity of *The Family Reunion*, relies a great deal on the devices of stage entertainment, amusing dialogue, unexpected twists of incident, delayed disclosures, and a slight air of mystification.

Reilly is shown as a hybrid between a psychotherapist and a religious director, as well as being head of a sort of private inquiry agency of which Julia and Alex are other members. These agents help to bring to a head the problems of the patients, the Chamberlaynes, Celia Coplestone and Peter Quilpe. Eliot has of course deliberately created an unrealistic role for Reilly, freeing himself from

the restrictions of using a naturalistic priest or psychotherapist, but bringing together in this role various possibilities of insight and influence. At times the agents'
function seems to be that of merely seeing and understanding the condition and possibilities of those around
them. Reilly and Julia, it is suggested, are both metaphor-
ically one-eyed and need each other to give a whole vision.
Julia, inquiring for her spectacles, says one lens is missing
and Reilly then sings of himself as the One-Eyed Riley.
Reilly says to Julia

> When I express confidence in anything
> You always raise doubts; when I am apprehensive
> Then you see no reason for anything but confidence.
> *Julia:* That's one way in which I am so useful to you.

And at the end Edward says

> Oh, it isn't much
> That I understand yet! But Sir Henry has been saying,
> I think, that every moment is a fresh beginning;
> And Julia, that life is only keeping on;
> And somehow, the two ideas seem to fit together.

And Julia perhaps describes her own role when she says
to Peter

> You must have learned how to look at people, Peter,
> When you look at them with an eye for the films:
> That is, when you're not concerned with yourself
> But just being an eye. You will come to think of Celia
> Like that, some day. And then you'll understand her
> And be reconciled, and be happy in the thought of her.

Reilly, however, goes far beyond observing and understanding; and unfortunately the mingling of functions in
his role leaves ambiguous at certain points the nature of
the influence he and his assistants exert on the patients.
The manipulation of the Chamberlaynes' party can be

said to be merely bringing to a head problems that had already half defined themselves to the patients; and when Celia makes her decision both Reilly and she emphasize that it is her own free choice. The two functions of being a seeing eye and of leading people towards the point where they can make their own clear choice are obviously compatible. But the Chamberlaynes, when they meet Reilly, receive such severe instruction from him that he evidently claims authority over them, as a religious director might, and when Alex asks

> The Chamberlaynes have chosen?

Reilly replies ambiguously

> They accept their destiny.

Their lack of real choice is emphasized by Reilly's taking responsibility himself for having sent them back to live out their lives together knowing their own and each other's meanness; he says of the decision

> To send them back: what have they to go back to?
> To the stale food mouldering in the larder,
> The stale thoughts mouldering in their minds . . .
> I have taken a great risk.

The fact that the ordinary people of the play are not given the same free choice as the potential saint seems an unnecessary weakness.

Reilly's handling of the Chamberlaynes is one with the slight complacency, the knowledgableness about spiritual things, that spoils the tone of some of the agents' speeches and arises partly from the hints of their undefined affiliations with higher powers. Obviously Eliot wished to keep alive a suggestion of the supernatural all through the play, and to fuse it with the mundane manipulations—telegrams to re-assemble the cocktail party, and so forth—that an ordinary detective agency could have managed. The danger is of a slight cheapness creeping in. It is hard, for instance, to see a serious purpose in Reilly's account of his original intuition (expressed in an apparition) that Celia was destined to a violent death. It seems beside the point: the significance of her choice was unconnected with the variety of death to which she was on her way, and presumably Reilly's help would have been equally available to such a person whether she was to die from violence or disease or old age. It seems to be one of the incidents that fills out the stage play without being required by the dramatic theme.

The lack of dramatic complexity that makes these things necessary is the outcome of a psychological over-simplification in the central argument. Eliot offers the view that only a small number of chosen or doomed people, the saints, like Celia, can take the course that leads towards selfless love, in the sense of love for something fully outside themselves. Apart from these few saints, everyone is relegated to the condition of the Chamberlaynes and the very possibility of a deeply satisfying human love is excluded without argument.

As in *The Family Reunion*, a contrast is drawn between love and the mutual dependence of psychologically un-weaned people. Edward Chamberlayne, speaking to the wife on whose domination he is dependent even while hating it, protests

> I may not have known what life I wanted,
> But it wasn't the life you chose for me.

And he tells Reilly about his condition when his wife returned to him after having, as he thought, left him:

> We had not been alone again for fifteen minutes
> Before I felt, and still more acutely—
> Indeed, acutely, perhaps for the first time,

The whole oppression, the unreality
Of the role she had always imposed upon me
With the obstinate, unconscious, sub-human strength
That some women have. Without her, it was vacancy.
When I thought she had left me, I began to dissolve,
To cease to exist. That was what she had done to me!

Reilly sees that this aggrieved dependence is associated
with Edward's incapacity for loving, and with his wife
Lavinia's incapacity for being loved, however much she
enjoyed controlling men. He says to them both

And now you begin to see, I hope,
How much you have in common. The same isolation.
A man who finds himself incapable of loving
And a woman who finds that no man can love her.

Reilly sends them away to make the best of a bad job, to
become reconciled to the low-level companionship that
they can give each other while they fulfil their conventional social roles. And this is all he holds out for anyone
except the saints; he says to Edward Chamberlayne

The best of a bad job is all any of us make of it—
Except of course, the saints— . . .

Celia, the saint, is aware of her solitude and the
illusoriness of the companionship that the people around
her seem to give each other. In contrast, until she understood Edward's incapacity for love, she had felt that what
they had together was completely right:

Oh, I thought that I was giving him so much!
And he to me—and the giving and the taking
Seemed so right: not in terms of calculation
Of what was good for the persons we had been
But for the new person, *us*. If I could feel
As I did then, even now it would seem right.
And then I found we were only strangers
And that there had been neither giving nor taking

> But that we had merely made use of each other
> Each for his purpose. That's horrible. Can we only love
> Something created by our own imagination?
> Are we all in fact unloving and unlovable?

With her realization that the love she thought they had was an illusion there comes a sense of sin described in words reminiscent of the phrase in *Murder in the Cathedral*: 'Emptiness, absence, separation from God.' Celia puts it,

> It's not the feeling of anything I've *done*,
> Which I might get way from, or of anything in me
> I could get rid of—but of emptiness, of failure
> Towards someone, or something, outside of myself;
> And I feel I must . . . *atone*— . . .

This is the condition Reilly is to cure, and he faces her with the choice between two possibilities. On the one hand there is the path of sainthood, without mutual human love, which she eventually chooses. The only alternative he can offer her is in effect a marriage like the Chamberlaynes', and this is taken as being so general that he calls it 'the human condition':

> If that is what you wish
> I can reconcile you to the human condition,
> The condition to which some who have gone as far as you
> Have succeeded in returning.

But he makes it very evident that this human condition is no more than a second best:

> They do not repine;
> Are contented with the morning that separates
> And with the evening that brings together
> For casual talk before the fire
> Two people who know they do not understand each
>   other,
> Breeding children whom they do not understand
> And who will never understand them.

Celia: Is that the best life?
Reilly: It is a good life. Though you will not know how good
         Till you come to the end. But you will want nothing
            else,
         And the other life will be only like a book
         You have read once, and lost. In a world of lunacy,
         Violence, stupidity, greed . . . it is a good life.

The dialogue between Reilly and Celia in his consulting room is, of course, the central statement of the play, and made so finely and forcefully that it can stand as a poem by itself. But it shows this weighting of the scales against any possibility of an approach towards full love between human beings without the illusions created by mutual projections. It avoids considering, for instance, the possibility that a woman with Celia's sensitiveness and accessibility to spiritual experience might have found someone less inadequate than Edward to fall in love with, and that they might have created a relation which remained part of the human condition without being as meagre as the Chamberlaynes'. The fact is that in the Chamberlaynes Eliot has shown people who, for all their decent intentions and ultimate achievement of humility in their role, are very severely crippled psychologically. They really do need psychotherapy rather than the talking-to that Reilly gives them. However common a condition their incapacity for giving and loving may be, it is not inevitable, it is not 'the human condition'. The false generalization by which the lives of these people are presented as the only alternative to sainthood such as Celia's makes the play psychologically less compelling and over-simplifies its basic dramatic structure.

The Confidential Clerk takes up three broad themes that have already appeared in the earlier plays: to put them very crudely, the relation of parents and child, the possibility of significant companionship in marriage, and the

discovery and the acceptance of one's identity and vocation. The parents in this play (like Lady Monchensey in
The Family Reunion) attempt to live by proxy in their
children, or in other ways to use them as instruments for
their own ends. Lady Elizabeth's effort to model Colby
into a son who will be a spiritual companion for herself is
a caricature of the real possibilities that are handled tragic-
ally in Lady Monchensey, and the extent to which Lady
Elizabeth approaches a conventional comedy figure suggests how thoroughly Eliot distanced the topic by his
treatment of it in the earlier play. Sir Claude, seeking the
companionship of a son, wants Colby to continue in his
life the mistake Sir Claude has made in his—of doing the
wrong job because he was better at that than he would
have been at his vocation. Mrs Guzzard, Colby's mother,
has tried to manipulate her son's life by depriving him of
the knowledge of his own undistinguished father and
giving him greater worldly opportunities as the supposed
son of Sir Claude; like Lady Monchensey, she has de-
prived her son of his father. And even Eggerson who,
according to Kaghan, was alone in not making the mistake
of wanting Colby to be something he wasn't, does in fact
hope and believe that Colby will become a priest instead
of sticking to his vocation as an organist. They all have
their plans for living the young man's life.

The main movement of the play is concerned with the
discovery of one's identity and the choice of vocation, and
it works up to Colby's rejection of the temptation Sir
Claude holds out of resigning himself to doing the wrong
job extremely well because he has no promise of distinction in his own proper job. The significance of loyalty to
one's vocation is emphasized by taking conventionally
uninspiring vocations: instead of being Father Damiens
or Albert Schweitzers the characters here are called to be
second-rate potters or organists. (In this respect, I imagine,

the play takes up the story of Peter Quilpe which *The Cocktail Party* left untold.)

In making his choice Colby gets crucial aid through discovering his identity, in the sense of learning who his father was. He says to Sir Claude

> You had your father before you, as a model;
> You knew your inheritance. Now I know mine.

The same discovery produces the climax of *The Family Reunion*, where the necessity for discovering the nature of the family curse that has to be expiated is the implied reason for its crucial importance. In *The Confidential Clerk* the need for a man to put himself into relation with his true father emerges as part of a claim, that runs through the whole play, for the vital importance of a natural parental relation, biological and psychological. Eggerson, whose son was killed, as anyone's may be, has suffered the natural grief but no loss of human dignity. Sir Claude, on the other hand, and Lady Elizabeth, who have for convenience half-abandoned their illegitimate children, are abject in their craving for the relation they sacrificed. Mrs Guzzard, too, concealed her real relation with Colby and, although she brought him up devotedly, pretended she was only his aunt; her fate is to know clear-sightedly that she has lost her old relation with him and can never now be psychologically his mother in spite of the biological fact. In the end the only parent-figure who effectually influences Colby's choice of vocation is his real father, dead before Colby knew him and apparently ineffective, who had not tried to modify his ordinary parental role and had got on quietly being the mediocre organist he had it in him to be.

Just as in the earlier play Harry's discovery of what his father was like and what he suffered allows him to see his way and free himself from emotional thraldom to his mother, so here the revelation of Colby's true father sanctions his choice of vocation, again with the effect of cutting off his mother's hopes. Whatever supernatural or quasi-biological significance the plays may assign to the disclosure of paternity, this dramatic theme is closely related to the important everyday fact that mother-dominated boys may find it difficult to assimilate what would be valuable to them of the father's qualities, and difficult to give him the loyalty from which they can draw strength to define themselves in spite of the mother.

All three of the modern plays deal with the experiences of separation and conscious loneliness endured by the person who accepts a vocation. And Eliot seems to suggest that such a character can no more have the companionship of sexual love if he is to work out his identity than he could retain the mutual dependence between himself and his mother. For Harry and Celia the possibility of love as anything more than a distraction and a delusion can hardly be considered. But *The Confidential Clerk* suggests and approaches a great change of outlook on this theme; a prominent and moving part of the play conveys the possibility that Colby and Lucasta may become deeply in love. In the love scene of Act II Colby speaks of his inner life as a garden, a garden that seems, like the outer world, partly unreal because he is alone in it, having neither religion nor human companionship. But as he and Lucasta explore their need of each other he recognises the possibility of finding after all, unexpectedly, that somebody has joined him in his garden:

> Walking down an alley
> I should become aware of someone walking with me.

The scene comes near to an affirmation of the possibility of intimate and satisfying companionship in love even for Eliot's hero.

The possibility, however, is not put to the test. It is evaded and the mode of evasion deserves attention for the bearing it has upon Eliot's practice of working at several levels simultaneously and combining the roles of commercial entertainer and serious dramatist. Instead of examining the possibility, for a man of Colby's quality, of sexual companionship at the same level of seriousness as vocational choice, Eliot resorts to the device, highly effective as theatrical entertainment, of allowing Colby to discover the seeming fact that Lucasta is his half-sister; with the result that he appears unaccountably to reject her and so pushes her back, baffled and angrily unhappy, into the arms of the simpler man Kaghan.

When in Act II Lucasta has said

> You don't seem to me
> To need anybody.

Colby's reply is clear and explicit:

> That's quite untrue.

After Lucasta's decision to marry Kaghan has been made, under what she regards as the salutary shock of Colby's rejection of her, she is made to say again

> Colby doesn't need me,
> He doesn't need anyone. He's fascinating,
> But he's undependable.

And to Colby himself she says

> You're either an egotist
> Or something so different from the rest of us
> That we can't judge you. That's you, Colby.

To this, still believing their kinship to be a barrier between them, he replies non-committally:

> That's me, is it? I simply don't know.

This dialogue in Act III obviously represents a great

change of attitude from Act II, the relinquishment of a moving hope on the part of each of them. Between the two states of mind there intervenes the entertainment device of the supposed incest barrier but no indication of serious experience that would form a compelling reason for such a change. Eliot presents once more, and without examination, his assumption that the destiny of those capable of the finest development involves the sacrifice of close companionship in sexual love. When later in Act III the incest barrier is shown not to exist Colby is made to to take the disclosure of his paternity only in its bearing on his vocation and not at all on his possible love for Lucasta. His relation with *her* has been got out of the way earlier, without his having had to face it as a real possibility. And this amounts to an evasion in one of the central themes of the play.

One of its consequences is that Eliot is not quite convincing about the satisfactory prospect for Lucasta of marrying B. Kaghan. After the possibilities hinted at in Act II it fails to ring true when she explains that what she really wants is security and conventional stability; it is difficult not to feel that she is ignoring qualities in herself that have previously been taken much more seriously. In other words, the handling of her experience too suffers because she is first shown as perhaps capable of achieving deep companionship with Colby, and then prevented by a theatrical incident rather than the demonstration of an intrinsic impossibility.

We might suppose that the aim of providing contemporary theatrical entertainment has at this point seduced Eliot from his more serious concerns, but it may be more accurate to say that in drawing back from a full examination of one of his themes he accepted the escape offered by the theatrical possibility of the incest misunderstanding. This is perhaps the chief danger of the double aim: the serious dramatist can shelve his unsolved problems by falling back on his role as entertainer. A psychological problem lurked in the unargued assumption that the type of person represented by Colby must at heart be lonely; a dramatic problem was posed by the fact that the theme of loyalty to one's vocation could not have been so effectively isolated and sharpened if Colby had been allowed to be fully in love with Lucasta. It is these problems that have been evaded.

*   *   *   *   *

The attempt to say what Eliot does in these plays leads in the direction of an assessment, at least to the extent of claiming that the plays are seriously concerned with experience of deep importance in human lives. They all deal with human loneliness, and with more facets of it than I have touched on (Agatha, for instance, in *The Family Reunion* and Sir Claude in *The Confidential Clerk*). They examine the bearings that parental relations, marriage, religious faith and the response to vocation have upon this central experience of loneliness.

The Family Reunion focuses on the necessity for ending a state of dependence between mother and child which has been so intense and prolonged as to prevent the child from establishing an identity of his own. It shows the hero discovering the possibility of love (but not, for him, human love) as an alternative to mutual dependence between two people. Associated with domination by his mother and failure in self-definition is his lack of an effective relation with his father; to know something of his father is an essential step towards Harry's release, and he is shown groping after this knowledge from midway through the play (in the scene where he and the doctor are at cross-purposes, the doctor preoccupied with the condition of Harry's mother, Harry preoccupied with his father).

153

The compassionate understanding of mistaken parents that reveals itself as part of Harry's growth when he has detached himself from his mother very evidently colours the treatment of parenthood in *The Confidential Clerk*; for one feature of that play is the gentleness of the demonstration that Sir Claude and Lady Elizabeth must not hope to find in an intense and intimate relation with a child the satisfactions they have failed to achieve in either marriage or vocation. From the child's point of view the emphasis has been shifted, as compared with *The Family Reunion*, from the mother to the father. The problem of relations with the mother was so decisively dealt with in the earlier play that now we have the episode in which Mrs Guzzard is made to ask Colby which parent it was the more important for him to discover—

You had no preference? Between a father or a mother?

—and Colby, with the brief reply

Let my mother rest in peace

goes on to formulate the relation he needs with a real father.

The development has been from the first urgent need in *The Family Reunion* to break an outdated bond with the mother to the hero's more constructive effort—more constructive, at least, in terms of human relations—to discover his father as a step in the process of achieving his own identity. This process occurs mainly as a recognition and acceptance of vocation, the discovery of the father serving to sanction the hero's choice; he gains strength to accept his proper role when he recognizes that his father had accepted his. The seeming suggestion that an urge to play the organ is transmitted in biological inheritance is a dramatic means of indicating that a man has a certain constitution with particular gifts and limitations—his 'fate'—which helps to determine his proper role. Hence the importance of Colby's identifying his real father and not accepting the substitute offered by Sir Claude.

In *The Family Reunion* the achievement of love and the acceptance of vocation are fused, and both are religious in form. *The Cocktail Party* gives a hint, in Celia's conception of the relation she had hoped she had with Edward Chamberlayne, that selfless love (love that is not self-projecting) might be possible between human beings. But it is no more than a hint, and Celia's achievement of love is again religious. So too is her vocation, though in Peter Quilpe the hint is given that the essential worth of response to a vocation survives the fact that the vocation may be far from religious; for Peter, 'making a second-rate film'. These are hints that *The Confidential Clerk* carries farther, in exploring possibilities of ordinary experience and human choice without explicit religious sanction.

In this last play, the topic of vocation is dealt with as confidently and decisively as that of the hero's need to find his father before he can establish his own identity. The changing treatment of human love, on the other hand, shows exploration but no settled conviction. *The Family Reunion* had taken for granted the failure in marriage of the mother-bound hero and made it a subordinate theme, a mere continuation for the hero of playing an imposed role, as he had been obliged to all through childhood, instead of being himself. *The Cocktail Party* had presented penetrating insight into the pathology of human relations that develops in the marriages and love affairs of the psychologically unweaned and of those who can love only their own personality. In that play too the man complains of having a role imposed on him, a life planned for him, by the woman. Their marriage is shown as capable in the end of becoming a disciplined and decent way of life for the two partners once they have accepted the limitations created by their psychopathology, in particular their incapacity for genuine love.

Now in *The Confidential Clerk* the possibility is affirmed, in Kaghan and the Lucasta of Act III, of a marriage in which there is mutual giving and receiving by a man and woman who have seen each other and not merely projections of themselves. Their values and needs, however, are kept very simple. A more profound development is hinted at in the relation of the Act II Lucasta and Colby: very tentatively Eliot approaches the possibility that people capable of subtle values might find in sexual love a companionship that contributed to their spiritual growth. Colby is a hero of more humility than Harry and Celia in that the possibility of human companionship while he creates his identity and fulfils his vocation is not absolutely ruled out. A stage trick allows it to be left unexamined. But this feature of the play, if it is as I think a flaw, may also point forward to a development in Eliot's work that has still to come. In *The Confidential Clerk* the assertion that the hero must necessarily accept some form of martyred loneliness has become less convincing, and less convinced, than it ever was in the earlier work. Eliot's plays have to be seen as a living structure, and, as in any living structure, the point of weakness and incompleteness is often at the same time the growing point.

A POSTSCRIPT ON 'THE ELDER STATESMAN'

The Elder Statesman takes up two ideas from the earlier plays, one from *Murder in the Cathedral*, one from *The Family Reunion*, and handles them with decisive differences. The differences are crucial in that they allow the new play to present the possibility of secure love between a man and a woman as something normal and realizable.

At the play's opening that possibility seems to be taken for granted, with Monica and Charles sure of each other and about to enter on an ordinary engagement. Then it appears that the engagement must hang fire. While her father lives he must come first with her. True, he is unlikely to live long, but his dependence on her is so great that while he lives she cannot let herself even become engaged and to that extent detached from him. The play unfolds the processes through which Claverton comes to the point of willingly releasing his daughter and enabling her to give Charles her full love without a divided mind or troubled conscience. In thus examining the problem of a parent who is over-dependent on a child, Eliot returns to the theme of Lady Monchensey and Harry of *The Family Reunion*. The change of the sexes is of small account; he has himself mentioned that even in the two-way traffic between an author and his characters, in the mutual development that occurs between them, a transposition of sex is no hindrance.

Lord Claverton's achievement in releasing his daughter affects him as well as her. She can marry feeling 'utterly secure' in her lover. Her father can accept his death in peace of mind instead of dying as Lady Monchensey dies, in defeat and desperate protest.

The Elder Statesman is the only one of Eliot's plays that strikes me as being more effective in reading than seen on the stage. A knowledge of Act III is needed before Acts I and II reveal their full meaning, and in the theatre, at least at first viewing, they have too little tension and complexity. The force and real nature of the threat to the lovers' happiness is not at all apparent in Act I. There it appears that although Monica is unwilling to get engaged while her father needs her, his rapidly approaching death will release her in a matter of months. It is not brought out clearly enough here that, if her father dies with his relation to her unchanged, not only will his life be unredeemed but her happiness in her eventual relation with Charles will be impaired. The seriousness of the danger springing from Claverton's dependence is too little brought out in Act I, and the sense of threat that should be there is missing. It is not until Michael's clash with his father in Act II that the damaging quality of Claverton's relation with his children comes out strongly.

Nor is the tension created by Gomez in Act I and by Mrs Carghill at the beginning of Act II fully adequate. Their behaviour too easily seems to be just eccentric and in bad taste, rather sinister certainly, but not the serious threat of disintegration it really is to the personality Lord Claverton has tried to create for himself. Only from the point where Michael appears, late in Act II, does the play come to reveal its pressures and complexities, to which the third Act then goes on to do full justice. Is it that the situation holds too little material for a three-act play? The thinness of the first two acts, compared with the dramatic compactness and richness of the third, would at first suggest that. But the probability is that what the first two acts lack is not material but a sufficiently clear indication of the developing themes, including perhaps something more on the significance of Claverton's failure to do all that might have been expected of him in public life. In reading the play one has the advantage of distributing attention according to the complexity of the theme, and therefore the thinness of Acts I and II matters less; they can be accepted as preparation for the last act. It is this last act, whether read or seen in the theatre, which possesses the quality of clarity with richness of meaning that marks the other plays.

The act ends with Claverton's death, a contented death, after he has found it possible to release his children, and especially to leave Monica to be happy with her lover:

The dead has poured out a blessing on the living.

Previously, unable to accept the person he is or the limits of his own being, he has been trying to live beyond himself through the lives of his children. Before his release he tells them

> You're all I have to live for, Michael—
> You and Monica.

Like Lady Monchensey, he places on his children the burden of justifying his life as well as their own, and he wants, as Michael sees, to extend it by proxy beyond its natural span:

> I was just your son—that is to say,
> A kind of prolongation of your existence,
> A representative carrying on business in your absence.

Claverton gains the power to release his children, and to release himself from them, by accepting the self he is. Previously he has filled a role, knowing that hidden parts of himself conflict with it. He has found it possible to interpose his role between other people and himself— 'Always his privacy has been preserved'—and part of Monica's task is to shield him from strangers during his retirement. Equally, she must keep at bay 'his terror of being alone', which has made him always need someone, usually Monica, to be in the room with him to receive an occasional remark, even while he works. His terror of being alone is his terror of the private self. Charles has

> sometimes wondered whether there was any . . .
> Private self to preserve.

And though Monica replies

> There *is* a private self, Charles,
> I'm sure of that.

she has no knowledge of what it is. He is, as we are later

shown, terrified of discovering in himself 'the hollow' or 'yellow' person that Mrs Carghill reports her friend Effie as having seen in him.

The denied parts of himself are symbolized by Gomez and Mrs Carghill, who demand to be taken up again as part of his life. They demand it with menaces, the insistent pressure of the hidden features of himself being represented by their blackmail. 'Why not leave Badgley and escape from them?' asks Charles, and Claverton replies

> Because they are not real, Charles. They are merely ghosts:
> Spectres from my past. They've always been with me . . .

They are in this respect like the Tempters of *Murder in the Cathedral* who bring Becket glimpses of his past phases and his present potentialities. The Tempters have something of the same tone, sinister in its assumed geniality, and something of the same perkiness of rhythm in their speech, as Gomez and Mrs. Carghill. To Becket they brought temptations that had to be resisted. He had to pass beyond them to greater austerity. For Claverton the healing process is exactly the reverse: he must accept Gomez and Mrs Carghill as part of his past life and forgive himself. What he has to pass beyond are not the faults but the savagely unforgiving judge within him:

> What is this self inside us, this silent observer,
> Severe and speechless critic, who can terrorise us
> And urge us on to futile activity,
> And in the end, judge us still more severely
> For the errors into which his own reproaches drove us?

Forgiving himself in private can never bring about Claverton's release. Eliot sees that communication is vital. The victim of the severe and speechless critic cannot help himself until he is sure of there being at least one person whose love is so complete that it can be trusted to survive the knowledge of all that he knows about himself; in other words, someone who is able to love him as he is and not only in the role he has built. As he approaches the point of confession he says to Monica:

> I've had your love under false pretences.
> Now, I'm tired of keeping up those pretences,
> But I hope that you'll find a little love in your heart
> Still, for your father, when you know him
> For what he is, the broken-down actor.

He had never been able to tell his wife of his concealed shames:

> I thought she would never understand
> Or that she would be jealous of the ghosts who haunted me.
> And I'm still of that opinion. How open one's heart
> When one is sure of the wrong response?

Claverton judges his own marriage in the light of the more complete and secure relation which might have been and which is now represented in the coming marriage of Monica and Charles.

Closely connected with that possibility of secure relationship is the attitude to faults and shames. Charles, speaking of his own past mistakes, is given a significant revision of words that Claverton suggests and that Charles momentarily accepts. Claverton asks him

> Has there been nothing in your life, Charles Hemington,
> Which you wish to forget? Which you wish to keep unknown?

He replies

> There are certainly things I would gladly forget, Sir,
> Or rather, which I wish had never happened.
> I can think of things you don't yet know about me, Monica,
> But there's nothing I would ever wish to conceal from you.

The close linkage is thus suggested between the ability to trust fully in another person's love and the freedom from an over-severe inner critic whose incapacity to forgive forces one to try to 'forget' past faults instead of remembering them as things one wishes had never happened.

Confession to someone secure enough, and completely enough committed, to be able to hear anything is the first step, 'And perhaps the most important', that Claverton takes towards his freedom. His full freedom is gained by facing his ghosts and no longer trying to run away from them. It is after that that he can say

> I've been freed from the self that pretends to be someone;
> And in becoming no one, I begin to live.

Claverton's process of release consists in the discovery that it is impossible to give and receive love unless one is reconciled to oneself, and Monica expresses his final attitude as well as her own feelings when at the end she says, in unashamedly emotional rhythm,

> Age and decrepitude can have no terrors for me,
> Loss and vicissitude cannot appal me,
> Not even death can dismay or amaze me
> Fixed in the certainty of love unchanging.

9

Reader and Author

THE spread of psychoanalytic ideas, some of them badly garbled, has raised a number of problems and pseudo-problems in literary criticism. No one now can doubt that an author's work may reveal features of his personality and outlook that he had no intention of expressing and which he may not notice unless his attention is drawn to them, or of which he may even be in the strict sense unconscious. Equally his work may stimulate unnoticed or unconscious processes in his reader and may be enjoyed or disliked partly because of its significance for preoccupations, preconceptions and inclinations which the reader may not recognize in himself. And since the less conscious implications may not be the same for the reader as they were for the author, or for one reader and another, uncertainties of communication arise. Among the apparent problems only some are real and only some are new. But certain familiar problems look more formidable nowadays, partly because of psychoanalytic ideas, and partly because of the obscurity of much serious writing, especially much poetry, in the last half-century.

The simple-seeming assumptions that the author should know what he means and do all he can to ensure that the reader knows too have been challenged. Apart altogether from what we know of the unconscious, it would by now have become evident that no knowledge of an author's conscious and paraphrasable intention would be decisive in defining our own view of his work. As T. S. Eliot writes in discussing Valéry's views on poetry:

He defends the privacy, even the anonymity, of the poet, and the independence of the poem when it has been written and dismissed by the poet. At this stage, the poet's interpretation of his poem is not required: what matters is what the poem means —in the sense in which a poem may be said to have 'meaning'. What the poet meant it to mean or what he thinks it means now that it is written, are questions not worth the asking. (Introduction to Paul Valéry, *The Art of Poetry*, London, 1948)

A first principle of criticism might seem to be, then, that the reader is concerned only with two things: the piece of writing as it is and his own mental processes in face of it. Knowing either of these things accurately is difficult enough, let alone making out what was in the author's mind. Attractive as that principle is, it has to be qualified if it is not to mislead. For to the extent to which either the author or the reader interprets the work in a private, idiosyncratic way, they have lost the implicit social link between them. This probably matters to the author; it certainly affects any reader who has come to suspect it. If what he enjoys in a work of art is unconnected with the artist's satisfaction, the work becomes an unintended feature of the world, non-social, like a sunset or a canyon, beautiful perhaps but not mediating contact with a human maker.

The social aspects of our enjoyment of any pleasing object matter all the time. Even in face of the natural or accidental object we want the sense of shared interest and sympathy, and we want it ideally from someone who not only agrees with us but whose own perception and evaluation are as sensitive and skilled as our own. And we want the response to be genuine—not "Tis very like a whale'. Even when we are by ourselves our enjoyments have the background of a social culture which we feel to be supporting or challenging or failing to understand our enjoyment; and even if we define our enjoyment, defiantly or regretfully, by its contrast with what others would like we are being influenced by them. We are inescapably social.

When an object is not natural but made, the social relation with our fellow-onlookers is accompanied by a social relation or quasi-social relation with the maker, even if he is unknown or dead. We cannot ignore what we suppose to have been someone's satisfaction in having made the object. Admittedly, we may be mistaken, but so we may be about any of our social relations: we misinterpret people's feelings even face to face, entice ourselves with supposed congenialities where there are none, get misled by resemblances to figures from our past, and create a social milieu of 'parataxic distortions' to use H. S. Sullivan's term, that are only gradually and never fully corrected as experience accumulates. There is nothing peculiar in a reader's misconceiving what an author has written. We are not, however, content to misunderstand; it comes as a disappointment to find that something we valued in an author is based on our own misreading. The fact that someone chose to make the work of art in the form we find satisfying, chose at least to the extent of letting it go as finished or publishable, is a vital element of our pleasure in it.

Suppose, for example, some later editor could demonstrate that Theobald's emendation was quite wrong and Shakespeare after all did *not* write of the dying Falstaff, 'his nose was as sharp as a pen, and a babbl'd of green fields', there would be disappointment. The phrase would be there still, as fine as ever; but the sense of communicating with Shakespeare through a shared satisfaction in it would be lost. Similarly with the modern cleaning of Canaletto's paintings: the revelation of sugary pinks and blues spoils—for those who find them disappointing—not only the cleaned pictures but the uncleaned too, for we have to recognize that our satisfaction in the subtler greyed colours may not have been a satisfaction Canaletto shared. What matters, for the social relation between the author and reader, is the author's satisfaction in his work, not his intention. What he intended to write at any moment prior to the arrival of the words is not of crucial importance; the question is what he accepted as part of his poem. It may have been lines composed by a friend, like Wordsworth's contribution to the description of the Ancient Mariner. Or it may have been a phrase that forced itself on him for reasons he could not consciously analyse. When that happens it is entirely possible that a reader may see more clearly than an author can—or bothers to see— what he has actually done in the poem. But still he has done it and accepted it as his. The important thing is not what the author, or any artist, had in mind to begin with but at what point he decided to stop.

What features of the poem contributed to his satisfaction with it—or at least to his willingness to leave it in existence as a work of his—may be hard to decide. Not everything that this or that reader thinks he sees in it may have had any influence on the author. Madariaga, for instance, claims as part of *Don Quixote* applications and extensions of meaning that have become possible only in the light of later history and must have been inaccessible to Cervantes. He writes of Don Quixote:

> Those very windmills and fulling mills which he fought, or meant to fight, have grown to be what his wild imagination fancied and seems to have guessed—giants of industry whose hundred powerful arms encircle the world, awe-inspiring powers which work in the night. Sancho's ambition to become the governor of an island has since then entered the hearts of the innumerable Sanchos who people the earth, so that, as there were not enough islands to satisfy so many would-be governors, and as, moreover, no natives were left to be governed, since even Sancho's Baratarian subjects had come to emulate the ambition of their lord, the matter had to be entrusted to enchanters. A

famous magician, by the name of Rousseau, succeeded in enchanting the Island Barataria in such a manner that all became at the same time governors and governed—and he confirmed this enchanted commonwealth with the fantastic name of Democracy. The which name, if Don Quixote in his scholarship would recognize it as meaning 'the power of the people', Sancho in his simpler common sense would certainly hold demoniacal and understand as 'the power of the devil'.

And thus, over earth and mind, three centuries of experience have passed, during which many an illusory castle has turned out to be an inn; many a beautiful Dulcinea has been enchanted into a rough and ill-smelling country wench. Religious unity in Europe, the American Eldorado, the dreams of the Age of Reason, the windmills of the Bastille, dream after dream and adventure after adventure—the ghost of Don Quixote has gone through since they laid his body to rest. Can we speak of him as did his contemporaries who saw him ride the plains of La Mancha? (Salvador de Madariaga, *Don Quixote: an Introductory Essay in Psychology*, Oxford, 1935)

This breadth of interpretative sweep holds a danger. When it goes so far that the attributed accretions of meaning are altogether beyond what the author could possibly have been aware of, we have lost the social relation between ourselves and him. Instead of feeling that when we contemplate the work of art we share in the author's satisfaction that it was as it was and not otherwise, we now have to recognize that he was only the initiator of a group process and that what we enjoy is a much later stage of that process. The work has become rather like a folk-product, and in grasping its accumulated meaning the reader is in a social relation only with the past of his culture, as he is in reading many of the nursery rimes, fairy tales, ballads, prayers and carols, and in understanding proverbs and established metaphors.

But when the work is known to be by one particular author it seems impossible to disregard the limitations of what he could have seen in it himself. Where we can see more modern applications of what he wrote we can no doubt fully accept them as part of the meaning his work would have implied if he had been writing later; we simply grasp in terms of our own institutions and familiar events what the author had understood in terms of institutions and events that had a parallel significance for him. Much of Voltaire's *Candide*, for instance, has this sort of contemporary relevance, and no doubt some of *Don Quixote*, as Madariaga claims. The question is where to draw the line, and the reader's practised judgment must be his guide in every instance. If we accept too much of the time-added meanings we are going in the direction of the medieval readers who claimed that a passage of Virgil was an unconscious prophecy of the birth of Christ; we depart too far from any meaning that the work could possibly have had for its author, and we lose the possibility of sharing in his satisfaction with the finished work.

The 'meaning' in this context is a complex matter, including as it does literal and symbolic statement and all the subtleties of attitude and emphasis conveyed by allusion, rhythmical reinforcement and contrast, and every other resource of writing. Difficulties arise when—naturally and inevitably—readers discuss the work with each other and hope to share their impressions of it. Any discussion of that kind means taking apart and approximately paraphrasing various constituents of the total meaning—in the same way, essentially, as people viewing a fine stretch of country point out this feature and that, the relation of one feature to another, the mood evoked by the light and so on. Our comments recreate neither the landscape nor the poem; but they serve to explore at least roughly the area of our agreement about the thing in front of us and to assure us that we are not entirely deluded in believing we share each other's interests and evaluations.

Difficulties occur only as we penetrate further into the subtleties of what we confront and into the processes of symbolism and association set going in our own minds.

Then it becomes a question how much we are educing from the poem itself and how much we are reading into it a construction of our own. Helen Gardner seems to construct something of her own rather than elucidate Eliot's meaning when she comments on the world's ending, in *The Hollow Men*, 'not with a bang but a whimper'. The poem is an extreme statement of Eliot's sense of the nullity and futility of much living, but Helen Gardner, having in mind the growth of religious feeling expressed in the next poems (five years later), suggests that we should understand the 'whimper' as being not only the note of ending but also the birth-cry announcing a new form of life. It seems extremely questionable whether that meaning, remotely possible as it is, can be plausibly tacked on to the end of a poem with the desolation of which it is so totally at variance. The same kind of doubt arises about some of the exegesis of Blake's poetry. Although J. H. Wicksteed is often illuminating (and always honestly explicit), his commentary, as I suggested earlier (cf. p. 34), sometimes imports a meaning—often of a conventionally Christian kind—into the poem, rather than drawing out a meaning contained there. Neither J. H. Wicksteed nor Helen Gardner gives any sign of drawing on technical psychology. They provide a reminder that the search for esoteric meanings and the extended interpretation of obscure poetry in the service of a preconception are not the exclusive privilege and temptation of those influenced by psychoanalysis.

The general psychological problem that outcrops here is that of the speaker's control of the listener's response. It might be called the problem of 'communication', but that term is misleading; it would suggest that some thought or idea had first been formulated and then expressed, a gross over-simplification of the process. That it is an over-simplification is clearest in a consideration of poetry, though it is true of very much writing and speaking. If we ask a poet what his poem is communicating we imply that he first had some idea or meaning and then translated it into the words of the poem. In fact what he had to say was not there until he said it. There was no preformed thought exactly corresponding to the poem but not the poem, any more than there can be an exact paraphrase which is not the poem. Eliot puts the point:

> We have to communicate—if it is communication, for the word may beg the question—an experience which is not an experience in the ordinary sense, for it may only exist, formed out of many personal experiences ordered in some way which may be very different from the way of valuation of practical life, in the expression of it. *If* poetry is a form of 'communication', yet that which is to be communicated is the poem itself, and only incidentally the experience and the thought which have gone into it. (*The Use of Poetry and the Use of Criticism*, London, 1933.)

This, however, is not a mysterious peculiarity of poetry. The same kind of caution, even if a less degree, is necessary in describing accurately what goes on in ordinary speech.

To describe speech as the communication of something is accurate in one context only: that is, when one has an actual verbal formulation already in mind and is in a position to decide whether or not to utter it to someone else. 'Communication' can accurately describe public utterance in contrast to verbally formulated private thought. It is paralleled by the writer's decision to publish a finished poem rather than leave it in his desk.

But the emergence of words or images as part of our total state of being is an obscure process, and their relation to the non-verbal is difficult to specify. They are not simply the expression of a state of mind; they are part of it. Even in ordinary conversation the phrasing of an attitude is sensitively keyed to the context in which we are speaking and—apart altogether from polite concealments and hypocrisies—the phrasing we adopt is part of the attitude we find we have taken up. To say this is not to accept the simple view of Watsonian behaviourism that thinking is indistinguishable from sub-vocal speech. Against this is the common experience of trying un-successfully to phrase a complex state of mind and having to say, 'No, that isn't quite what I mean'; when that happens the verbal formulation is evidently not fully con-sistent with some other non-verbal aspects of the dis-criminations and attitudes which are emerging, and we go on groping. At the other, and equally unacceptable, extreme from the early behaviourist view lies the naïve separation of thought from speech that led to the metaphor of finding words to clothe the thought, and to the ideal of writing 'What oft was thought but ne'er so well ex-press'd'. This latter view is unacceptable if it implies that there could be alternative phrasings of the same thought, but acceptable if it points to the ideal of finding one fully accurate and adequate expression of all that lurks within the 'thought'.

The words we choose (or accept as the best we can find at the moment) may obliterate or slightly obscure or dis-tort fine features of the non-verbal background of think-ing. Some people are unaware of this because they speak or write so fluently that thought processes apart from words seem scarcely to occur; the verbal moulds are ready to shape their thinking from the start. The more easily the established (or fashionable) language usages and clichés are accepted, the less evident will be any non-verbal aspects of thinking. A subtler use of language often consists in breaking and reshaping the more familiar verbal moulds. I have tried earlier to indicate (see above, p. 108) that some of T. S. Eliot's poetry, for instance, is a way of expressing a concept for which no word exists. But in a simpler way a great deal of speaking and writing involves the effort to be a little more faithful to the non-verbal background of language than an over-ready acceptance of ready-made terms and phrases will permit.

The non-verbal aspects of thought, the emergent definitions of interest, awareness of task or intention, perceptual discriminations, images, half-grasped similarities, shades and contrasts and conflicts of attitude, part-activated sentiments, suspected relevancies of information, these are not to be called pre-verbal. For in all probability language plays a part almost from the beginning of the process. Words are available, aiding definition or tempting towards distortion, from the earliest stages of thinking; for many people they are as promptly available as non-verbal imagery. Far from serving merely to 'express' thought they are one of its elements and a constituent part of the total pattern of inner behaviour that thinking is. In fact it may happen that the words finally emerging possess ambiguities or obscurities that preserve features of the inner behaviour denied by the intended statement. Slips of the tongue or pen such as Freud interpreted and some of the ambiguities examined by Empson have this function, and I have drawn attention to the evidence in some poetry that the manipulation of language may help to create the thought that it seems to 'express' (see p. 99 on Rosenberg, and cf. Shelley's use of language in *Adonais*, discussed in the following essay, p. 187).

Great differences obviously occur in the extent to which writers allow the less defined and less well controlled meanings and associations of words to affect what they finally write. The Augustans differed strikingly in this respect from the Romantics and still more from some of the twentieth-century poets. So too writers differ in the degree to which they use simple 'emblems' or more indefinite 'symbols' (cf. above, p. 74). The more they depart in either respect from a clear nucleus of approximately paraphrasable meaning the greater the uncertainty in their control of the reader's response and the nearer the approach to a chaos of idiosyncratic readings with every reader enjoying (or disliking) a different poem. Some individual differences in reading will necessarily occur owing to diversities of individual experience and private associations to words and events. But unless a large nucleus of the poem is public property, with an intelligible meaning agreed about by those readers whose capabilities bring the poem potentially within their reach, we shall have lost the bond between author and reader and between one reader and another. And these bonds are vital, for— as the history of Blake's poetry, for instance, shows vividly —a literature is not just a sequence of authors but a growing social structure of which readers form an integral part.

Needless to say there is nothing wrong with completely idiosyncratic interpretations of anything, poems, pictures, music, clouds or coal-fires. But if that is all we want there is no need of authors and artists; we could just as well take a benzedrine tablet and sit down with a Rorschach blot or a picture from the Thematic Apperception Test and let our imagination loose. Understanding in the reader and intelligibility in the author are essential to a literature and involve obligations in both. The tasks are not peculiar to literature; obscurities and misunderstandings are common enough after all in everyday speech, where speakers fail to say just what they mean to say and listeners fail to grasp what seems clear. Giving and taking wrong impressions are part of social existence. Failing to get the response we hope for from our hearers is admittedly a failure in speech, and can scarcely be counted a success in literature, whether it results from the author's failure to guide the reader's response sufficiently or the reader's failure to take the guidance. Although there are sound reasons for denying that the writer 'communicates' something that existed apart from the communication itself, still he communes with the person for whom he writes and, if they are to share the poem, the necessity remains for him to guide and control the reader's response.

In doing this he can offer only the verbal component of a pattern of inner experience the totality of which includes much else besides words and articulate thought. The reader reconstructs from the verbal component as much as he can of the rest of the pattern. In gesture language the hand in a downward clasping position may represent 'old age', being the fragment from which convention allows the observer to reconstruct a bent old man with his hand clasping the stick he leans on. In complex verbal language, conventions, associations and context interact with incalculable intricacy and subtlety to allow us to reconstruct from the verbal fragment a large part of the unspoken pattern. The question for intelligibility, in literature or speech, is whether enough of the verbal component of the author's experience has been given and whether it is effectively enough articulated with the rest of the experience to guide a competent reader in the direction the author intends. The 'reader' may in fact be the author himself at a later date, or immediately after a first attempt at formulating his experience; and the inadequacy of words to carry with them enough of the state of mind of which they formed part is an all too common observation.

10

The Hinterland of Thought

THERE is a passage in *Troilus and Cressida* in which Ulysses, describing the big brotherly aptitude of the State for spying out private affairs, implies that thoughts are not full-grown from the start but have their origin and infancy:

> The providence that's in a watchful state
> Knows almost every grain of Pluto's gold,
> Finds bottom in the uncomprehensive deeps,
> Keeps place with thought, and almost, like the gods,
> Does thoughts unveil in their dumb cradles.

The nature of those dumb cradles, the area where thought emerges from what is not thought, raises questions, of interest beyond technical psychology, that have been comparatively neglected by psychologists—and perhaps neglected by most people who had been trained to make as promptly as possible for the precise formulation of thought in words.

I

When psychologists have worked explicitly on thinking they have been concerned mainly with the processes by which we refer to things without their being perceptually present. These are what Stout called 'free ideas', processes allowing of the covert rehearsal of possible experience, freed from perception and overt action. The intimate neuromuscular nature of these processes will presumably remain unidentified, except in general terms, for a very long time. In experience, however, they appear most clearly in the form of images and words, though less easily detected processes also occur, those that preoccupied the psychologists of the Würzburg school. Among these less obvious processes the most readily observable is 'task orientation' or 'set', the process that tends to filter out ideas apparently not relevant to the aim we have adopted, and which also seems to have a selectively osmotic action, drawing in ideas that are relevant.

The eventual petering out of the Würzburg work, amidst headshakings over the fruitlessness of the controversies it provoked, is fully understandable in the light of the fact that those psychologists were following an introspective route into a limbo between thought and not-thought where introspection, being itself thought, must eventually fail. Their achievement in going as far as they did was remarkable.

What might be called the Würzburg processes form, therefore, one frontier of articulate thought. They can be observed mainly when we try to solve problems which we have already defined or had presented to us in cognitive terms.

II

Much of our thinking is not of this kind. It consists rather in the recognition of our own motives, the exploring of our interests, the formulation of desires and intentions, the definition and re-definition of attitudes and preferences. Bodily states of need and of conflict between needs, states of contentment, satiety, discomfort, gradually make their way into awareness, where they appear as more or less specific desires and attitudes. On their way towards formulation all these impulses are brought into some degree of relation, tangential or intimate, with possibilities revealed by present perception, with memories of past occasions and premonitions of consequences, with conceptual systems, sentiments, moral codes, rules of logical thought and so on.

Both the emergent impulses and the processes that modify them may exist in modes far different from words or imagery, these latter forming a late stage of their definition. Their more rudimentary existence is seen most clearly in expressive movement. That includes not only facial expression and the obvious patterns and changes of posture but also much finer postural sets and movements: shrinkings, local tensions, twistings, asymmetries of muscle tone, and also contractions of smooth muscle in the viscera and changes in the circulatory system. We know from the observations of Wolf and Wolff that the gut can blush and blench like the face. Behaviour of this kind, much of it extremely difficult or impossible to detect even if we try to attend to it, may be the only way in which beliefs and evaluative attitudes exist—doubting, welcoming, fearing, suspecting, confiding, resisting, protesting and so forth. The man whose habitual expression is supercilious, or distrustful, or apologetic, is making a statement of belief about himself in relation to other people, though he may not hold the belief in verbal form. If psychoanalysis or psychotherapy brings it to verbal formulation or other ideational recognition he may be dismayed to find he harbours such a belief or expectancy and may mobilize other beliefs to counteract it. At times the physical behaviour expressing beliefs and attitudes contributes to psychosomatic disorder. In the ordinary way it simply comprises the intimate gesturing of the whole body, which may accompany or precede or entirely replace the out-cropping of a belief or attitude in cognitive terms.

In ways like this, emergent impulses may undergo evaluation and perhaps modification in the light of our value systems before they reach conscious formulation. In speaking of value systems I mean the whole structure of our needs and interests, all the directions in which we are responsive to the environment, together with the whole structure of sentiments or systems of attitude which influence our evaluation of particular situations. The nonconscious control of impulse by a value system occurs in a simple, obvious form in, for instance, the control of bladder functions during sleep or in psychogenic impotence—cases where impulse conflicts with some system of values, whether expressed in habit or repressed, and is inhibited by processes outside consciousness. The same type of organization which here results in simple inhibition can in other cases bring about other modifications of impulse, such as allowing it expression accompanied by a sense of guilt or followed by depression.

Psychologists and physiologists have still not fully explored the extent to which, in this sense, the body thinks. It concerns us here because it shows that an emergent impulse can be brought into relation with value systems long before imaging or verbal thinking occurs. It follows that by the time an impulse has flowed over into imagery or words there has been ample opportunity for it to be checked, facilitated or modified by processes outside consciousness. It comes gradually to definition, filtered through at least some part of the array of values that constitutes the person.

To speak of the body as thinking, in this sense, does not imply the so-called peripheral theory of thought, or the James-Lange theory of the emotions; nor does it commit me to a belief in subception. I am suggesting something much more generally accepted though perhaps not much attended to, and I must enlarge on it a little.

We know that in the ordinary perception of everyday

life any number of things are briefly perceived and
neglected; and that some of them, though not thought
about, activate processes resulting in later thought activity:
it may be a dream, incorporating day remnants, it may be
a memory image of some place interrupting our reading
of a book and sometimes traceable to an association with
words we had read a page or two back, it may be the solution of a problem in which the neglected percept plays a
vital part (as in Maier's pendulum problem). The neglected
percepts have not been repressed, though they have
worked at unconscious levels. They will all have emotional
significance, being at least in some slight measure welcome
or unwelcome—we can agree with Magda Arnold that
emotion completes sense perception—and therefore the
full behaviour involved in the perceiving will certainly
include bodily processes. Suppose for instance those are
slight fear responses: they occur in an organism with
established attitudes towards fears (attitudes of courage,
timidity, denial, for instance), and these attitudes too are
partly bodily, taking the form of shrinkings, bracings,
neck movements that alter the position of the chin, twistings of the shoulders, to mention easily observable possibilities. There may also be temporary moods, these again
consisting partly in bodily states including general mus-
cular tonus and levels of blood pressure. There can be no
reason to doubt that interaction between the perceptual
response with its emotion and the modifying mood or
trait (the anxiety state, for example, or the courage given
by trust in one's companions) may begin at the physical
level. If we really believe in the organism as a psycho-
physical whole and not as a body bossed by a mind we can
hardly deny that a great deal of organization and mutual
modification of impulses can go on in bodily terms
whether or not it eventually appears as cognitive experience.

III

The images and words that the writers and readers of a literature encounter may therefore carry with them the results of extensive organization occurring before they made their appearance. The appearance of images and words is what Susanne Langer describes as the symbolic transformation of experience; she regards it as a characteristically human function and one that occurs spontaneously and incessantly, not merely under the spur of some other need. She writes:

> Speech is, in fact, the readiest active termination of that basic process in the human brain which may be called *symbolic transformation of experiences*. The fact that it makes elaborate communication with others possible becomes important at a somewhat later stage. Piaget has observed that children of kindergarten age pay little attention to the response of others; they talk just as blithely to a companion who does not understand them as to one who gives correct answers. Of course they have long learned to use language practically; but the typically infantile, or 'egocentric', function persists side by side with the progressively social development of communication. (*Philosophy in a New Key*, London, 1951.)

Langer emphasizes the fact that a word or image (or of course a sequence of them) may carry a number of meanings simultaneously. The meanings are related to one another but they are not given the sequential ordering that marks logical speech, nor are the relationships stated explicitly. She speaks of 'presentational symbolism' to distinguish this kind of imperfectly differentiated thinking from the array of explicitly related ideas that she calls 'discursive thinking'. This presentational symbolism is a fact familiar enough. One day when I was making notes for this essay I had a phrase or two from Chopin's socalled Funeral March perseverating as auditory images.

They expressed the day's general mood of slight depression; I was also weary with various departmental ex-
asperations and the tune meant 'Tir'd with all these, for
restful death I cry'; but the more cheerful resurgent tune
and tempo of the second movement was also lurking
somewhere and conveyed a secret denial of the general
mood, an obscure assertion that things would still be all
right. Put into ordered thought it amounted to saying,
'I'm depressed and gloomy because of all these irritations
and interruptions to what I want to do, but although it
feels like the end I suppose there's still an undercurrent
of happier possibilities, and if there isn't, well, the worst
that can happen is death and there's a lot to be said for
that.' There was no need for these thoughts to be formulated in serial order, or for both bits of the tune to go
through my head: a phrase or two was enough to ensure
the partial activation of processes that could become
thoughts if I stopped to think. The presentational symbol
was not merely a way of expressing these incipient attitudes and ideas but an indication that they had come into
relation with one another long before they reached
articulate thought.

A half-way house between presentational symbolism
and discursive statement is to be seen in some of the
torrential passages of Shakespeare where half-activated
images succeed one another with great rapidity and gain
their effect through not being brought to the full definition of an exact metaphor. The *Macbeth* passage about
Pity like a naked new-born babe is an obvious example.
The sense of the passage is that in spite of the seeming
helplessness of any protest against the horrors perpetrated
by unscrupulous power, the decent human emotion of
pity can in the end mobilize enormous strength. But
Shakespeare stopped long before this stage of discursive
statement. He had in mind presumably a mass of items

and associations related to the central theme: the new-born babe as an example of extreme helplessness, the cherubs on maps blowing the winds, the immense power of the wind and the fact that it brings tears to the eyes—and they could be tears of pity—especially if it blows something into them, the way it rushes all over the world like an invisible messenger carrying heaven's protest against the crime, in other words carrying pity, which in spite of being a helpless infant is now in charge of the tremendous strength of divine as well as human condemnation of the crime. And all this that I fumble after comes tumbling out quite briefly:

> And pity, like a naked new-born babe,
> Striding the blast, or heaven's cherubin, horsed
> Upon the sightless couriers of the air,
> Shall blow the horrid deed in every eye,
> That tears shall drown the wind.

What a passage like this reveals is not disorder but a complex ordering of attitude and belief achieved a stage earlier than discursive statement.

IV

In a stimulating, patchy book published in 1924 and almost unanimously neglected ever since, L. L. Thurstone suggested that it mattered very much how early on in its progress towards definition an impulse was brought into relation with other impulses and value systems. In the duller individual and the more limited species, he thought, a motive has to come very close to definition—perhaps be fully acted out in the external world—before it is brought into effective relation with conflicting impulses or environmental obstacles. The characteristic of the brighter person and the more complex species is to have resources for organizing its impulses at a further remove from overt behaviour.

Starting with the familiar notion of a gradation from organisms with only contact receptors, through those with distance receptors, and on to those capable of anticipating and covertly manipulating possibilities that are not perceptually present, Thurstone suggested extending the same scale further and using it to differentiate degrees of human capacity. Though all except grossly defective human beings can imagine possibilities of action before being committed to them, there are differences in the promptness with which the incipient impulse to act is considered in relation to its imagined outcome and to the effect of that outcome on the person's other needs and values. Long before intelligent people commit themselves to action, long before even an intention is fully defined, the originating impulse will have been modified by relevant systems of interest and sentiment. As this implies, Thurstone insisted that intelligence is not limited to cognition but also involves an ordering of our motives. He put the gist of his view in these terms:

> The less there is of the impulse at the time when it is subject to rational acceptance or rejection, the higher is the mentality of the actor. Genius is essentially the capacity to deal effectively with impulses at the stage of formation when they are still only roughly affective states, before they have absorbed enough attributes to become the cognitive terms with which most of us are limited in our field of rational control. (*The Nature of Intelligence*, London, 1924, p. 84.)

Thurstone believes that the complete psychological act consists in a motive defining itself to the point where it issues in some overt action. Consequently we cannot say precisely what the impulse or motive is until it has been acted out. Every act is slightly different from every other and in Thurstone's view this means that every motive is slightly different from every other. If we choose to say that several different actions may be alternative ways of satisfying the same motive we must then mean by motive something which is broad and in one sense very little defined. We may for instance need fluid, but the ways in which we finally satisfy the need are exceedingly various. If we consider one of the earliest attempts at the psychological selection of military personnel, that reported of Gideon, we can see that whether his thirsty soldiers went down on their hands and knees and lapped, or whether they scooped the water up in the palm of their hands made no difference to the satisfaction of the very broad need for fluid, but did represent two very different patterns of total motivation, one overwhelmingly dominated by thirst, the other showing a fusion between thirst and an alert concern for safety. In more everyday thirst-quenching there are almost infinite variations in the final act, according to the beverage chosen, whether we take a cup or a glass, whether we reject it because it is chipped, has been used by somebody else, and so on. In all the cases the total pattern of motivation is slightly different and is only defined by the overt action in all its unique detail.

This implies that the definition of the motive depends on environmental opportunities—the details of the stimulating situation—as well as on internal states. Psychology, Thurstone thinks, studies the succession of processes from metabolism through thought to perceived stimuli and eventually conduct. 'We have to study,' he says, 'the manner in which the individual goes about hunting for the stimuli that the environment does not immediately give, the manner in which his dynamic self finds overt expression through and by the stimuli that happen by chance to be available, and his compromises with substitute stimuli which in other moments he would reject as inadequate.' True of ordinary concrete behaviour, this account applies with even more obvious aptness to the emergence of thought into words. The less sensitive writer skids from the potentially new thought into the fluent old words, accepting a compromise which burkes what might have been an original creation.

V

The scientist or any writer committed to the ideal of literal statement must of course carry as much as he can of his emergent thought right through to the stage of discursive statement with an explicit definition of the relations between items. All that he says we can expect him to be aware of and to have meant. Against the background of such psychological thinking as Thurstone's, however, it seems clear that a writer, especially a poet, using words, images and incidents with evaluative or symbolic overtones is likely very often to convey meanings which he can't be said to have intended before writing and which he may not observe even when he reads over what he has written, a possibility of which Empson in particular has illuminated many aspects.

What may well happen is that a more or less accidental turn of phrase satisfies the poet because it happens to convey a part of his total state that he was not aware of and not intending to express. Wordsworth and Shelley, for instance, seem at times to create a complex or subtle effect through what looks like an accident in the words they use; it happens especially when overtones or ambiguities in the words enrich what would otherwise have been a much simpler statement. Wordsworth draws attention to one example of it in his own work, because he provided a later revision which put more clearly what he consciously intended to say but which also eliminated everything that made the original lines interesting. It occurred in the

Elegiac Stanzas Suggested by a Picture of Peele Castle,
where he wrote the famous lines:

> Ah! THEN, if mine had been the Painter's hand,
> To express what then I saw; and add the gleam,
> The light that never was, on sea or land,
> The consecration, and the Poet's dream.

In his deadened years he changed this (though on a correspondent's urging he later restored the original). The revision ran

> . . . and add a gleam
> Of lustre, known to neither sea nor land,
> But borrowed from the youthful Poet's dream.

The revision undoubtedly gives a meaning that fits better with the later stanzas, in which the Poet's dream is seen less as a consecration than as an illusion and in which Wordsworth speaks of submitting himself to 'a new control'. The revised version conveys a slight disparagement of the Poet's dream, especially as he now becomes 'the youthful Poet'. The original wording in contrast suggests the intense value the Poet's dream still had for Wordsworth despite his effort to change his conscious point of view; it reveals a saving division of mind, a valuable flaw in the reasoned case. And, further, the original wording gives a half-impression of a mysterious natural phenomenon, 'The gleam', 'The light that never was'—something defined only by a negative. The revision, 'a gleam Of lustre, known to neither sea nor land', reveals itself much more promptly as being only a metaphor for a subjective psychological quality. It seems as though the 'accident' of word arrangement in the first version half-suggests that the poet's vision is a quality of the world of nature outside him. Stated explicitly, that idea would have conflicted too evidently with Wordsworth's main intention in the poem; hinted at through the words' overtones, it gives extra complexity of sense to the lines and adds itself in a shadowy way to the explicit thought that was being stated.

Verbalizing seems to be a two-sided process in which both sides are simultaneously active. On the one hand human experience includes an infinite variety of shades and patterns of feeling, attitude, desire, interest and discrimination. On the other hand language provides a vast range of subtle ways by which to refer to such experiences. When we speak or write, experience in some way merges with, and emerges in the form of, patterns of language. But in some minds the language processes reflect not only the main experience, in statements that could be more or less paraphrased, but also much subtler features of the non-verbal experience, and features of which the writer may have no awareness except through the overtones of what he finds himself writing. Even then he may well fail to notice what he has said.

VI

I find it difficult to distinguish clearly between confusion and complexity in this context. Though we can say that complexity implies a coherence and reconciliation among the diversities it brings together, yet in particular cases and especially when many-faceted and only partly conscious themes are in question it may be hard to decide. That problem comes up, as one would expect, in some of Shelley's work. And I should like to examine briefly an example I discussed some years ago,[1] where accidental turns of phrase bring to light facet after facet of an underlying theme of incipient thought which is very uncertainly related to the explicit statements Shelley seems to be making. It occurs towards the end of *Adonais* where he is trying to come to terms not only with the death of Keats

[1] 'Shelley's Poetry', in *The Pelican Guide to English Literature*, vol. 5.

but with the fact of death itself. His central and explicit idea is that Keats had, through death, achieved union with the universal and eternal spirit:

> Dust to the dust! but the pure spirit shall flow
> Back to the burning fountain whence it came.

And his death is not to be lamented:

> He hath awakened from the dream of life—
> 'Tis we who, lost in stormy visions, keep
> With phantoms an unprofitable strife.

From this point of view, the life we know is a sort of contamination:

> From the contagion of the world's slow stain
> He is secure.

But beneath this explicit, abstract conviction there lie conflicting attitudes, and they get their chance to emerge because Shelley is not only stating an idea but contemplating it in relation to a particular event and in a particular setting. The setting is Rome and the Protestant cemetery. He is reminded first that intellectual works survive their creators, and he adds to the thought of Keats's reunion with the Eternal a belief in the survival of his works in earthly life, among those other

> kings of thought
> Who waged contention with their time's decay,
> And of the past are all that cannot pass away.

Earthly life has begun to reassert its claims. The phrase 'time's decay' turns him to its fascinating and partly attractive aspects in the ruins of Rome,

> at once the Paradise,
> The grave, the city, and the wilderness,

in which also the sunlit Protestant cemetery with flowers in the grass provides another contrast between death and the pleasantness of continuing life. In the stanza describing it an appreciative reference to the ancient monument of Caius Cestius introduces the idea of the long survival of a *material* memorial in great beauty, and so diminishes still further the original concentration on the Eternal.

Next, because the grave of Shelley's son is also there, he voices the ordinary human sense of grief in bereavement, very different from the high-flown rejoicing of Keats's entry into the Eternal, and then, abruptly, he breaks into his own sense of protest at the world and presents death as a matter neither for grief nor for rejoicing but regressively as a refuge from the pains of living:

> From the world's bitter wind
> Seek shelter in the shadow of the tomb.

Immediately afterwards he switches back to the original theme:

> What Adonais is, why fear we to become?—

but the switch back at this point adds a very different emotional tone to the notion of reunion with the Eternal and in the very form of the question admits the fear of what has just been regressively welcomed, the fear being emphasized a little later with the line

> Why linger, why turn back, why shrink, my Heart?

All through these stanzas Shelley has been bringing up various attitudes to death, not all of them compatible with one another. In the next, crucial stanza, the last I want to examine, he opens with a reaffirmation of the original theme, very explicit (and poetically very much shop-soiled)—

> The One remains, the many change and pass;
> Heaven's light for ever shines, Earth's shadows fly.

But when he goes characteristically on to explore further among the possibilities of light and eternity he produces the much more interesting statement

> Life, like a dome of many-coloured glass,
> Stains the white radiance of Eternity,
> Until Death tramples it to fragments.

Those lines bring together with great compression his two main conflicting attitudes. The crucial word is 'stains', with its double meaning: it suggests a stain blemishing the radiance of eternity (like 'the world's slow stain' which Keats escaped), but it equally suggests the colourful interest of life, which interposes itself like a dome of stained glass between the pure spirit and the burning fountain whence it came. And where Shelley's nominal theme would demand that the colours of life should gladly re-combine to find fulfilment in the white radiance, the attractiveness of life in all its differentiated colour is emphasized by the suggestion of brutal destructiveness in the way it ends:

> Until Death tramples it to fragments.

The contrasting and sometimes barely consistent ideas in these stanzas seem to have reached expression partly through verbal associations that might be called accidental, were it not that they evidently gave openings for important variants of idea and attitude to emerge. 'Time's decay', which the kings of thought defy, leads to a contemplation of material decay in the Roman ruins; the monument to Caius Cestius, called a 'refuge' for his memory, later produces 'the shelter of the tomb'; the tears and 'gall' that await us in life suggest the world's 'bitter' wind that immediately follows. In this way the partial surrender to the seeming accidents of language has become a means of discovering and releasing partly-formed ideas and attitudes, not a tool for 'expressing' them after previous sifting. And if we feel that in the earlier fluctuations of his attitude towards death Shelley gives evidence of confusion, there is a good case for arguing that in the last of these stanzas he achieves very real complexity, and especially through the crucial use he makes of the word 'stains'.

The facts have been summed up by Paul Valéry when he describes the composition of *Le Cimetière Marin* and speaks of 'my attempts, my gropings, inner decipherings, those imperious verbal illuminations which suddenly impose a particular combination of words—as though a certain group possessed some kind of intrinsic power . . . I nearly said: some kind of *will* to live, quite the opposite of the "freedom" or chaos of the mind, a will that can sometimes force the mind to deviate from its plan and the poem to become quite other than what it was going to be and something one did not dream it could be.' (*The Art of Poetry*, London, 1958.)

VII

We can say, then, that when an author is satisfied with his work, or content to leave it as finished, many of the causes of his satisfaction will be in some sense 'unconscious'. But in what sense precisely has to be examined.

There is first the familiar psychoanalytic idea that unnoticed associations of ideas or ambiguities may let out something the author would not have suspected himself of meaning. Those apparent accidents of expression by which the censor is evaded do occur, but they are not the most interesting features of unconscious activity if we are concerned with the gradual emergence and formulation of ideas. The idea that evades the censor is generally one that is quite clearly defined and could have been verbally formulated if it had been acceptable. In exploring the significance of slips of the tongue and free associations the analysts usually illuminate not the matrix of ordinary thought but fully formed and often very simple thoughts which are dissociated from the organized personality. It makes for confusion in this context that Freud included within the one notion of the unconscious not only repressed ideas which could perfectly well have been conscious and introspectable if they had been tolerable but also the processes he called the Id which never can be introspected. His scheme might have been less confusing if he had treated the pre-conscious as emerging from the Id and kept his term 'unconscious' for repressed and dissociated material.

We are still obliged to use similes and metaphors in describing these things, and I think the metaphor of distance as well as depth is needed. We stand at the harbour of our mind and watch flotillas of ideas far out at sea coming up over the horizon, already in formation of a sort; and though we can re-order them to a great extent on their closer approach, we cannot disregard the organization they had before they came in sight. They are all submarines, partly under water the whole time and capable of submerging entirely at any point and being lost to sight until analytic techniques undo the repression. But it constitutes a fundamental difference whether an idea is out of mind because it has been forced to dive or because it has not yet come up over the horizon. Sometimes repressed ideas may be close in-shore, forming the co-conscious that interested Morton Prince. Others may be both under water and at a great distance; they find expression in some sorts of dreaming, especially the sorts that have most interested the Jungians. And in creative work great numbers of ideas, more or less organized, are simply out of sight beyond the horizon and can be brought into view only through the redispositions we make amongst the in-shore mental shipping that we *can* see and control.

The main emphasis of Freud's work was on the unconscious that has been formed by repression and it was Jung who gave more attention to the emergence of ideas out of the remote distance of the non-mental. In his elucidation of dream-work Freud identified the overdetermined symbol, one combining multiple meanings, which seems very likely to be a possible way by which at an early stage of thinking potential ideas are held in a common matrix without being organized through articulate relationships. But Freud attributed it to 'condensation', implying that defined ideas (whether or not repressed) have been brought together; there is in the dream, he says, 'an inclination to form fresh unities out of elements which in our waking thoughts we should certainly have kept separate' (*An Outline of Psycho-Analysis*, Ch. 5). The alternative view that certain symbols are the undifferentiated totalities out of which clear ideas may emerge, each representing only an aspect of the whole, has been put forward with great insistence by Jung in his doctrine of archetypes. It seems to me a matter for regret that because of Jung's quality of mind symbols of this kind should have been given that name and made to seem more mysterious than most thinking.

I imagine Susanne Langer felt the same, for a great deal that she says about 'presentational symbolism' is closely allied to Jung's ideas, and yet she never mentions him and refers instead (and in my view misleadingly) to the Freudian process of condensation.

VIII

Jung makes it clear that the archetype is something that emerges into mental form from the physiological remotenesses that lie beyond the horizon of mental processes. He writes that 'The symbols of the self arise in the depths of the body and they express its materiality every bit as much as the structure of the perceiving consciousness. . . . The more archaic and "deeper", that is the more *physiological*, the symbol is, the more collective and universal, the more "material" it is. The more abstract, differentiated, and specific it is, and the more its nature approximates to conscious uniqueness and individuality, the more it sloughs off its universal character. Having finally attained full consciousness, it runs the risk of becoming a mere allegory which nowhere oversteps the bounds of conscious comprehension, and is then exposed to all sorts of attempts at rationalistic and therefore inadequate explanations.' (*The Archetypes and the Collective Unconscious*, London, 1959.) Without trying to decide whether Jung meant by the collective unconscious something very mysterious or something very ordinary, we can accept his basic notion of the gradual emergence toward articulate ideas of a more undifferentiated cluster of processes, including physical processes, a cluster which may be highly coherent and capable of piece-by-piece expression in organized, articulate thought—though it may be so nearly inexhaustible in potential meaning that, as Jung says, no conscious formulation ever does it full justice.

The difficulty I find in accepting Jung's full idea of the archetype is the implication that the image itself which conveys the meaning arises from the depths or remotenesses of the body. For instance some sense of surging animal vitality and its huge potential power may arise in any of us and may emerge into conscious experience from below, in the way that the experience of hunger emerges out of bodily processes. As it comes towards 'symbolic transformation' the most appropriate image to hand may be, or may have been for many centuries past, the horse; and the horse may then serve as the symbol of a very complex mass of inarticulate potential experience, including a sense of the delight, the danger, the power, the vulnerability, the wildness and the manageableness of animal vitality. But although the meaning of the symbol may have come towards definition out of the remotenesses of the whole psychosomatic person, the image—the horse —seems most likely to have entered by way of the sensory surfaces, especially the eye.

There seems no good reason for restricting this line of thought to the highly charged symbols that Jung called the archetypes. Symbols of less profound and extensive significance may show on inspection the over-determination and multiple meanings which can be seen in one of two ways—as the result either of condensation or of the emergence into focal definition of a selection of ideas belonging to a whole cluster of potential ideas that may perhaps never become conscious in its entirety.

The choice of objects to carry the symbolic meaning may be largely an individual matter, or it may be culturally institutionalized, and it is of course an important concern of writers and some other artists. It seems likely that very early and perhaps infantile perceptions (or later percepts that have partly fused with them) may often be used in trying to convey experience that is highly important but difficult to define. Some of the deep significance that we attach to landscape may well be of this kind. Without assuming rather mechanically with some of the Freudians that the mountaineer is scrambling on his mother's breast we can still accept the likelihood that contours of the land do dimly suggest bodily lines and masses that must at one time have been of supreme importance to us. The notion has presumably often been used in paintings; Ivon Hichens puts it explicitly in paintings that fuse a landscape composition with a reclining nude. More interesting in our context is a passage by Wordsworth which seems to suggest that very early and very vague percepts may have contributed to the meaning that landscape had for him.

It occurs in *The Prelude* immediately after the much-quoted passage about his borrowing a boat without permission and being terrified by the impression that a huge black peak was striding after him, the externalization of a grimly punitive super-ego. What follows, though I believe it receives less attention from critics, is intensely interesting. The boyish experience ushered in a quite remarkable state of mind:

> but after I had seen
> That spectacle, for many days, my brain
> Worked with a dim and undetermined sense
> Of unknown modes of being; o'er my thoughts
> There hung a darkness, call it solitude
> Or blank desertion. No familiar shapes
> Remained, no pleasant images of trees,
> Of sea or sky, no colours of green fields;
> But huge and mighty forms, that do not live
> Like living men, moved slowly through the mind
> By day, and were a trouble to my dreams.

These unknown modes of being seem like a very primitive, perhaps infantile, form of awareness in which figures and objects have very few discriminable features and yet are charged with immense emotional significance, in this case of a threatening kind. Although the passage is a retrospective report, after a long interval, its unexpectedness, almost oddity, gives it an appearance of truth; it sounds quite different from the rather sententiously reflective lines that introduce the whole episode. Wordsworth himself has no explanation of the state of mind; he makes no comment on it. He implies only that whatever these vast forms were, their meaning had become fused with that of natural objects like his retributive peak.

Rather than give more examples from literature I must briefly summarize my argument. I suggested that the

Würzburg psychologists went as far as introspection could take them in examining non-verbal and non-imaginal processes which may occur when we mobilize ourselves to solve a problem that has already been formulated; but psychologists have given less adequate attention to the thinking that consists in defining our needs, desires and attitudes. Freud came close to it in his work on dream mechanisms, but he was preoccupied almost entirely with the disguise of what could have been fully formed thoughts, rather than with the gradual definition of thought out of something less articulate. This latter process was much more the concern of Jung; his description of the archetypes puts in cosmic terms facts about the presentational symbols in which incipient thought processes reach a very early stage of organization. Something of the same ground has been covered by Langer and generalized beyond the particular symbols that Jung calls archetypes. But the most useful framework for discussing these problems is offered by Thurstone's notion that organization may be introduced at an early stage into processes that precede articulate thought, and that consequently thoughts may sometimes be very extensively ordered before they are accessible to logical control. We know very little about the precognitive ordering of incipient thought, but I suspect that we could find out more about some of its features by exploring more extensively, by such techniques as electromyography, the intimate postures and expressive movements of the body. Meantime, as one would expect, the creative writers provide examples of nominally discursive statement which shows on inspection some of the characteristics of presentational symbolism and at times traces of a richer matrix, perhaps more confused, perhaps more complex, from which their words and images have emerged.

THE END

INDEX

198